Maria French

Verba Verbi Dei

The Words of Our Lord and Saviour Jesus Christ

Maria French

Verba Verbi Dei
The Words of Our Lord and Saviour Jesus Christ

ISBN/EAN: 9783337167240

Printed in Europe, USA, Canada, Australia, Japan

Cover: Foto ©Lupo / pixelio.de

More available books at **www.hansebooks.com**

Verba Verbi Dei

THE WORDS OF OUR LORD AND SAVIOUR JESUS CHRIST

HARMONIZED BY

THE AUTHOR OF "CHARLES LOWDER"

WITH AN INTRODUCTION

"Fiat mihi secundum verbum Tuum"
"Et Verbum caro factum est, et habitabit in nobis"

LONDON
LONGMANS, GREEN, & CO.
AND NEW YORK: 15 EAST 16th STREET
1894
All rights reserved

FRATRI AC SORORIBUS

AMANTISSIMIS

FAUSTA OMNIA PRECANS.

CONTENTS

	PAGE
INTRODUCTION	ix

FIRST PERIOD.

PRIVATE LIFE OF JESUS CHRIST .   1

SECOND PERIOD.

THE BEGINNINGS OF THE MINISTRY OF JESUS CHRIST .   5

THIRD PERIOD.

FIRST PUBLIC MINISTRY IN GALILEE.

PART I.

TO THE DEATH OF ST. JOHN THE BAPTIST .   15

PART II.

FROM THE RETURN OF THE TWELVE APOSTLES TO THE CLOSE OF THE GALILÆAN MINISTRY .   53

FOURTH PERIOD.

JUDÆAN MINISTRY.

PART I.

FROM THE DEPARTURE FROM GALILEE TO THE FEAST OF DEDICATION   73

PART II.

FROM THE FEAST OF DEDICATION TO THE LAST PASSOVER   97

FIFTH PERIOD.

	PAGE
THE GREAT WEEK .	125

SIXTH PERIOD.

THE GREAT FORTY DAYS	189
THE WORDS OF OUR LORD FROM HEAVEN, RECORDED IN THE ACTS OF THE APOSTLES	197

INTRODUCTION

THE following pages contain by no means a Harmony of the Gospels, but only of the words spoken by our Lord Jesus Christ. They fulfil a desire long felt to see those words alone, separated from all narrative. This can, of course, only be profitable to those familiar with the narrative; but there are times, especially in weakness, when mind as well as body seems unable to take nourishment except in a concentrated form, and when we feel that even the continually recurring "And they say unto Him" adds to brain-fatigue, and we desire to hear His words alone.

It was necessary occasionally, in dialogues, to give the words of others, but this has been done as briefly as possible, and in italic type.

The same words of our Lord (or nearly) given by different Evangelists on the same occasion are not repeated, but those which seemed fullest and most forcible have been chosen, a sentence being often composed of parts of verses from different Gospels, the light which they cast on each other being thus, as it were, gathered into one focus.

In all cases, however, references are given to the Gospels of which the words are *not* in the text, so that all the versions of our Lord's words on any occasion may be readily compared; and it is hoped that to the young and unlearned this may perhaps cast some fresh light upon the words, issuing in greater adoration of Him who spake them. The points of light, like the sparkle of a sunbeam upon dew, may come out more brightly by being brought close together, especially if we turn to the references, and observe the numberless ways in which this occurs; such as, for instance, St. Luke alone mentioning that before choosing the Twelve our Lord continued all night in prayer,[1] and also that He was "alone praying" before asking the great question,—the answer to which was to form the foundation of His Church.[2]

A few words are needed as to the order in which our Lord's utterances are placed. A certain framework of time and place is desirable, lest, if these be forgotten, much of the force of His words be lost. They are too often read without realizing the circumstances under which they were spoken; such as the period of His earthly ministry, and whether to the people of Galilee or to the doctors of the Law at Jerusalem. "The peasantry of Galilee," Bishop Westcott wrote, "that 'warlike race,' as Josephus describes them — who had in earlier times withstood the chariots of Sisera, and were yet again to vindicate their independence

[1] St. Luke vi. 12.
[2] St. Luke ix. 18. The first allusion to His second coming seems also to be in St. Luke's Gospel (xii. 36).

against the arms of Rome—still clung to the literal faith of their fathers in simplicity and zeal. They wished to raise Jesus to an earthly throne, and led Him in their Paschal train to the Holy City.[1] Their religion lay in action, and their faith in obedience." To them, "whether at Capernaum or Jerusalem, we find the truths of Christianity addressed in their plainness and active power. Parables and maxims are multiplied to enliven their apprehension and direct their energy."[2]

An attempt has therefore been made, in this little work, to indicate time and place in connection with our Lord's words; though with earnest desire to express no certain opinion on many points concerning them where the wisest differ. Some framework was needed, and pains have not been spared in studying the results arrived at by some of the best and most learned harmonizers of the Gospels. But if any kind readers should be led to study the subject for themselves, and arrive at different conclusions from the writer, the following pages will not have been put forth in vain; for, indeed, to draw any heart to deeper thoughts on the Life and words of our Lord is the very object with which they have been compiled. They do not profess to be critical, and it is hoped they may chiefly be used devotionally.

Amongst books on the subject, the latest—the great work of Père Didon, to whom all students of

---

[1] St. John xii. 12-19.
[2] "Introduction to the Study of the Gospels," pp. 265, 266. Macmillan and Co.: 1860.

the Gospels are deeply indebted—has been of the most essential use to the writer.

The division of our Lord's ministry into periods of a year, reckoning from Passover to Passover, has not been adopted, as being arbitrary rather than following the lines of distinct epochs in that ministry which appear in the Gospels. Until these epochs are clearly grasped, we must miss much of great importance in the history which is of the deepest concern to mankind. The times at which His words on earth were spoken are here divided into six periods—

I. From the Teaching in the Temple to the Temptation of JESUS.

II. From His return from the desert (St. John i. 29), shortly before the first Passover in His public life (St. John ii. 13), A.D. 27, to His going up to Jerusalem for "a feast of the Jews" (St. John v. 1), February, A.D. 28.

III. From the imprisonment of the Baptist (February, A.D. 28), and the beginning of the great Galilæan ministry, to its close, by our Lord's final departure from Galilee for Judæa during the Feast of Tabernacles, in October of the same year.

IV. From October, A.D. 28, to the Last Passover, April, A.D. 29.

V. The Great Week.

VI. The Forty days after the Resurrection.

Before each of these periods a table of our Lord's journeys to and fro has been prefixed, so far as they can be gathered from the Gospel histories of that period; and also a table of the principal events that fell within those limits, whether any words of Jesus are recorded in connection with such events or not.

In Holy Week the events of each day are given separately.

———

A few remarks may add clearness as to the second, third, and fourth of these periods.

1. As regards Period II. It seems generally thought now, by the best authorities, that "a feast of the Jews" (St. John v. 1) was not the Passover of A.D. 28, which is mentioned further on (St. John vi. 4), and at which there is no account of our Lord being present, but probably that of Purim,[1] which fell in February. This period would therefore last about ten months (from April, A.D. 27, to February, A.D. 28). The only record of these months is in the Fourth Gospel[2]— the record of the beginnings of His ministry—what may, perhaps, be called His semi-public life, before the voice was silenced which was still preparing His way.

The most ordinary student of the Gospels must feel the difference between the history of these ten months, and of those which follow them—the kind of domestic tone which pervades the narrative of this period; the Baptist's loving testimony to Him as he sees Him coming to him at Bethabara after the forty days in the desert; the four or five disciples gathering round the Lamb of God—abiding with Him that day, and called with Him and His mother to the marriage-feast; the little touch which tells so much

---

[1] See Esth. ix. 26–28. [2] St. John i. 29—v. 47.

in the words, "After this He went down to Capernaum, *He and His mother;*"[1] Nicodemus seeking Him at night, when the primary law and basis of His kingdom is privately declared; His discourse alone by the well-side to the Samaritan woman.

This hidden ministry, if we may call it so, is indeed openly manifested, almost at its commencement, by His outburst of zeal for His Father's house at the first Passover after the Baptism, A.D. 27, and it ends, nearly ten months later, with the inauguration of His general ministry at "a feast of the Jews" (taken to be that of Purim) at Jerusalem, by His open declaration that He was equal to the Father. "Therefore did the Jews seek to kill Him"—the first note of the tragedy to be accomplished two years later, in consequence of the same assertion. But, having borne His first open witness to this truth in the centre of religious life, He departed from it on hearing of the imprisonment of the Baptist.[2]

2. As regards Period III. The only serious difference of opinion regarding the dates given above is as to the end of the second and the beginning of the third period. It is clearly marked in the Gospels: 1. By the imprisonment of St. John Baptist, upon which our Lord left Jerusalem for Galilee (St. Matt. iv. 12; St. Mark i. 14), and by "a feast of the Jews" (St. John v. 1). It seems generally agreed now, as has been said above, that this feast was not the Passover of A.D. 28; but some still suppose it to be the Feast of Pentecost in A.D. 27, *i.e.* May 30, in which case the

---

[1] St. John ii. 12.   [2] St. Matt. iv. 12.

third period mentioned above would have lasted from June, A.D. 27, to October, A.D. 28. But with Kepler, Tholuck, Wieseler, etc., "a feast of the Jews" is here taken to be that of Purim, which fell in February, A.D. 28.

At this point the narratives of the three synoptic Evangelists begin.[1] They omit the record supplied by St. John of the time—a distinct era in our Lord's public life, and sharply divided from all which preceded and followed it—between the Baptism and the opening of the great Galilæan ministry.

His holy precursor disappears, alone with God in the dungeon of Machærus, as he had been alone in the desert; his last recorded words declaring that his joy was fulfilled in hearing the Bridegroom's voice. "He must increase, but I must decrease." His place was left vacant, and He Whose way he had prepared comes forth as a bridegroom out of his chamber, and announces, "The time is fulfilled." The period which thus began, probably of eight or nine months, closes with His final departure from Galilee for Jerusalem, not long after the Transfiguration. Beginning (according to the reckoning here adopted) after the Feast of Purim (February or March, A.D. 28), it ended in October of the same year, when the Feast of Tabernacles,[2] for which He went to Jerusalem, took place. It comprises the story of the evangelization of Galilee, and, when its distinctly marked boundaries are realized, we can the more readily follow the august history of the great Light shining

---

[1] St. Matt. iv. 12; St. Mark i. 14-16; St. Luke iv. 14, 15.
[2] St. John vii. 2, 10.

on "the people which sat in darkness, by the way of the sea, Galilee of the Gentiles." Slowly, and with the calm of dawn, the Sun arose over the Galilæan hills, and for a season all evil things gat them away together, and lay them down in their dens.

"The kingdom of heaven is at hand," are His first words, and He chooses to lay the firm foundations of that kingdom amidst the rural population of Galilee, rather than at the jealously guarded centre of Jewish Law, and of the traditions with which it was encrusted.

In spite of its great memories and energetic patriotism, Galilee, which had neither doctors nor schools of fame, obtained no consideration in those times of formalism and religious legality when all credit was given to the scribes and masters of the Law. The inhabitants of the metropolis, and Jews of pure race, despised her. The Galilæan was to them uncultured, ignorant, simple, and rude; they ridiculed both his dialect and his accent.

Yet the kingdom of Christ was founded and organized during those brief months in Galilee—that kingdom which shall never be destroyed, but which shall break in pieces and consume other kingdoms, and shall stand for ever.[1] The apparent poverty of the means is out of proportion with the immensity of the results, and this contrast forms the greatest enigma of history. He Himself is the key to it; in Him is contained the whole Divine idea expressed in the words, "the kingdom of God," and every word and act

---

[1] Dan. ii. 44.

of His life is in relation to it. "If He preaches, it is to publish the good tidings of the kingdom, and explain what it is; if He teaches upon the mount, it is to promulgate its laws; if He speaks to the people in parables by the lakeshore, it is to show them in outward images the mysteries of the kingdom, its origin, evolution, struggles, and victories; if He multiplies miracles, it is to prove that He is its Founder and Master; if He is transfigured before some of His disciples, it is to show them what humanity becomes in that kingdom." And He died "to overcome, through death, the obstacles which hindered its establishment."[1]

The evangelization of Galilee has a markedly popular character; yet even there, it must have aroused gravest difficulties, since all, in the Person and doctrine of Jesus, was opposed to the prejudices of the people and their teachers, who expected a political rule, and a Messiah crowned with earthly might.

The story of this period falls naturally into two parts—that of His early fame and popularity, culminating in the feeding of the five thousand; and that which begins with the great discourse at Capernaum,[2] the crisis of His ministry, when He openly declares that the miracle which had raised His reputation to its highest point is but a shadow of the great mystery by which, until His coming again, He should feed His own. He is immediately disbelieved and forsaken by many. "Will ye also go away?"

---

[1] Didon's "Jésus Christ," vol. i. p. 261.   [2] St. John vi.

He asks of His chosen ones; and from that moment a sadness falls upon the Gospel narrative, and the clouds gather thick and dark which were to break in the tempest of the Passion. "Woe unto you!" is spoken to each city where He had taught; the enmity of the Pharisees to whom further signs are refused is intensified; and His coming sufferings and death are twice predicted. Even in the glory of the Transfiguration the discourse is of His decease.

3. There can scarcely be a difference of opinion as to the beginning and end of the fourth period of our Lord's life, from the final departure from Galilee (St. John vii. 2-10), in October, A.D. 28, when He went up to Jerusalem for the Feast of Tabernacles, to His returning to the Holy City for the Last Passover, in April, A.D. 29.

The days which brought joy to the human heart of Jesus are over—those "dawn-golden days" when the people glorified God, saying that a great Prophet was risen up among them, so that the rumour of Him went out throughout all Judæa. The gleams of brightness in His earthly ministry are over, and when He left Galilee and journeyed to Jerusalem, it was to enter on an unceasing conflict with cavillings, misrepresentation, blasphemy, rejection—a struggle in which the last six months of His earthly course were spent, amongst those whose unbelief, prejudice, and hardness of heart resisted even Him. Far different from the state of the Galilæan peasantry was, Bishop Westcott writes, "the state of those Jews who had been brought into contact with Greek intellect or

Roman order. For them new regions of thought were opened which seemed to indicate that religion was only for the wise. They felt the full difficulty of founding any universal earthly sway, and either rejected the Messianic hopes as results of fanaticism, or saw in the course of things around them the signs of some mighty spiritual change which should more than fulfil the metaphors of the ancient prophets." [1]

As we read and consider the story of this period, the sense grows upon us of the tremendous struggle of the great Teacher with the moral force around Him, and with the unseen foe whose bitter and furious inspiration is so apparent in the words—very mutterings from hell—of his mouthpieces. Through the gloom of those last days, as "the Royal Banners forward go," we see the ranks of the enemy gathering for the battle, in which seeming triumph was to issue in everlasting defeat. And as at the close of the Galilæan ministry He permitted His veiled glory to break forth on Tabor, so, at the end of the sad months in Judæa, He manifested, by His greatest miracle, His glory as the Conqueror of death and of corruption.

We owe the history of these six months almost entirely to the two latter Gospels, the narrative being taken up by St. Matthew and St. Mark only at the last journey to Jerusalem, in March, A.D. 29.[2]

The above short and imperfect notices may perhaps be of use to some by bringing distinct epochs of our

---

[1] "Introduction to the Gospels," pp. 265, 266.
[2] St. Matt. xix. 13; St. Mark x. 13.

Lord's ministry more clearly into connection with His words. When we see them alone, we are the more impressed by their fewness. "The magnificent temperance of genius" is always one of its qualities; but what temperance of the kind equals that of the record of His words in Whom were all treasures of wisdom and knowledge? Amongst all utterances, Divine or human, they must ever stand alone, since they are the words of Him Who was perfect God and perfect Man. He, One with the Father and the Holy Spirit, had, in that eternal and ineffable union, spoken to man from his creation. "The Lord said unto me," and "Thus saith the Lord," were the prophetical preludes to God's words to man. They were from God alone, not from God made Man; for the Word had not yet taken flesh, and dwelt among us. "Holy men of old spake as they were moved by the Holy Ghost;" "All Scripture is given by inspiration of God;"—beyond this the Church has not defined the mystery of God's words to men.

But she speaks, since the message to Mary and her response, with a voice as of a trumpet ringing through all the world, of the perfection of both Divinity and humanity in Him, the great Martyr, Who only broke the silence of His Passion to declare that He was God and King, and Who died because of the assertion, which His judges heard from His own mouth.

His words stand therefore alone as those of One absolutely perfect in humanity, Who is God. Not, as seems sometimes vaguely held, as though His

Divinity, infused into a human body, constituted His soul; for then He would not be, for ever and ever, perfect Man. His words, most human in their pathos and tenderness as well as strength, are the expression of a perfect human soul, as truly as they were uttered by the human voice of Him Whom His disciples heard, saw with their eyes, and Whom their hands had handled. But they are informed by omniscience, since they are the words of God. "Never man spake like this Man," because never had man and God been one Person. Alas! in Christian England, how often is He thought and spoken of "not simply and consistently as God, but as a being made up of God and man, partly one and partly the other, . . . or as a man inhabited by a special Divine presence;" and as though "He became the Son when He was conceived of the Holy Ghost."[1]

We have heard of the thrill which passed through the listeners to those quiet discourses in Adam de Brome's Chapel, which were the seed of the greatest religious movement for centuries in Christendom, when, after dwelling on the indignities of the Passion, Dr. Newman said, "Now I bid you remember that He to Whom these things were done was Almighty God." And there is no power to realize, however faintly, the awfulness and the comfort of His words until the total and personal union, without confusion, is held of the human nature and the Divine nature which "gave His words the expression of the one perfect human Soul;" "all His

[1] See "Discourses to Mixed Congregations," by Cardinal Newman, p. 346.

human faculties," to use the words of a theologian on so great a mystery, "receiving from union with the Divine nature a plenitude and harmony which make Him the finished type of man. Ignorance does not limit His thought, and error never ruffled it. Inspiration in Him is constant; not, as with the prophets, a borrowed and intermittent gleam, but the infinite light, the ever-beaming rays of the Eternal Word."[1]

And yet His words are full of natural influences around Him. If the most gifted souls are those in which the profoundest harmonies exist with the scenes amidst which they have grown up, what must the natural beauty of His Nazarene home have been to its Creator, beholding it with human eyes? There He saw with admiration the anemones, lilies, and tufts of asphodel—the carpet of wild flowers which, we are told, is nowhere so fair as in the early spring of Palestine; the fig tree putting forth its green figs; the fields whitening for the harvest; the vines pruned that they might become more fruitful; lost sheep straying, flocks brought back to the fold. There He saw the jackals gain their lair,[2] the eagles and vultures gather together to their prey; the red glow of the morning and evening sun, betokening fair weather or storm, and the swollen torrents undermining houses without foundations.[3]

A few words, in conclusion, from the great work to which the writer is most of all indebted may be permitted: "Born a Jew, in an era of marked character-

---

[1] "Jésus Christ." vol. i. p. 96.   [2] St. Matt. viii. 20.
[3] See "Jésus Christ," vol. i. p. 87.

istics, Jesus resembles none of the geniuses of His people, ... neither the Hebrew doctor Hillel, nor the Hellenist Philo. His words, His doctrine, recall nothing of either the one or the other. He is Himself. What He says is of all time, as living to-day when eighteen centuries are past as when spoken. His work embraces the whole of what is eternal and essential in humanity." "The word of man, however great it be, cannot attain such sublimity and intuition—making for itself a road to the very heart of humanity—penetrate the future with such certainty, and engrave itself so profoundly in the memory of mankind, that, after long ages, it should be found still echoing and ever living upon the lips of those who adore, pray, suffer, love, and hope."[1]

PULHAM ST. MARY THE VIRGIN,
   St. Matthias' Day,
      MDCCCXCIV.

[1] "Jésus Christ," vol. i. pp. 106 and 77.

FIRST PERIOD.

THE PRIVATE LIFE OF JESUS CHRIST FROM A.D. 9.

From the Passover in April, A.D. 9, *to February,* A.D. 27.

THE JOURNEYS OF OUR LORD RECORDED IN THE FIRST PERIOD.

From Nazareth to Jerusalem . . .	*St. Luke* ii. 42.
Return to Nazareth	*St. Luke* ii. 51.
From Nazareth to Bethabara	*St. Mark* i. 9.
From Jordan to the Wilderness of Judæa .	*St. Luke* iv. 1.

EVENTS RECORDED IN THE FIRST PERIOD.

The Finding in the Temple . .	*St. Luke* ii. 41-50.
The Baptism .	*St. Matt.* iii. 13-17.
The Temptation	*St. Matt.* iv. 1-11.

VERBA VERBI DEI.

The Child Jesus with the Doctors in the Temple.

JERUSALEM.

April, A.D. 9.

His Mother. Thy father and I have sought Thee sorrowing.
How is it that ye sought Me? wist ye not that
I must be about My Father's business? *St. Luke* ii. 49.

The Baptism.

BETHABARA.

January, A.D. 27.

To St. John the Baptist.

Suffer it to be so now: for thus it becometh us
to fulfil all righteousness.   *St. Matt.* iii. 15.

The Temptation.

WILDERNESS OF JUDÆA.

The devil. If Thou be the Son of God, command that these stones be made bread.

It is written, Man shall not live by bread alone, but by every word that proceedeth out of the mouth of God. *St. Matt.* iv. 4.

The devil. If Thou be the Son of God, cast Thyself down.

It is written again, Thou shalt not tempt the Lord thy God. *St. Matt.* iv. 7.

The devil. If Thou therefore wilt worship me, all shall be Thine.

Get thee hence, Satan: for it is written, Thou shalt worship the Lord thy God, and Him only shalt thou serve. *St. Matt*. iv 10.

(Cf. *St. Luke* iv. 3–12.)

SECOND PERIOD.

THE BEGINNINGS OF THE MINISTRY OF JESUS CHRIST.

From His return to Bethabara from the desert, shortly before the first Passover of His public life, April, A.D. 27, to His going up to Jerusalem for a Feast (St. John v. 1), in February (?), A.D 28.

JOURNEYS OF OUR LORD RECORDED IN THE SECOND PERIOD.

From the Desert to Bethabara beyond Jordan
    St. John i. 28, 29.
From Jordan to Cana in Galilee with the First Disciples . . . . *St. John* ii. 1.
To Capernaum with His Mother . . . . . *St. John* ii. 12.
To Jerusalem for First Passover after His Baptism, *April*, A.D. 27 . . . . *St. John* ii. 13.
From Jerusalem into the Land of Judæa . *St. John* iii. 22.
To Sychar . . . . *St. John* iv. 3, 5.
To Cana of Galilee . . . . *St. John* iv. 46.
To Jerusalem, for a Feast . . . . . . *St. John* v. 1.

PRINCIPAL EVENTS RECORDED IN THE SECOND PERIOD.

The Meeting of Jesus and John the Baptist . *St. John* i. 29.
First Call of Four Disciples . . . *St. John* i. 37, 40, 41, 43.
First Miracle at Cana . . . . *St. John* ii. 1-11.
First Passover after the Baptism . . . *St. John* ii. 13.
First Cleansing of the Temple . . . . *St. John* ii. 14-16.
Miracles . . . . *St. John* ii. 23.
The Visit of Nicodemus . . . . *St. John* iii. 1-21.
Evangelization of Country-part of Judæa . *St. John* iii. 22.
Conversion of the Samaritan Woman and Citizens of Sychar . . . . *St. John* iv. 5-42.
Healing of Nobleman's Son: Second Miracle at Cana
    St. John iv. 46-54.
Healing of Impotent Man at Bethesda . *St. John* v. 2-16.
First Declaration of His Being and His Mission at Jerusalem . . . . *St. John* v. 17-47.

Call of the First Disciples.

BETHABARA BEYOND JORDAN.

March (?), A.D. 27.

To St. Andrew and another.

What seek ye? *St. John* i. 38.

St. Andrew and another. Master, where dwellest Thou?

Come and see. *St. John* i. 39.

To St. Peter.

Thou art Simon the son of Jona: thou shalt be called Cephas, which is by interpretation, A stone.

St. John i. 42.

To St. Philip.

Follow Me. *St. John* i. 5, 43

Of Nathanael.

Behold an Israelite indeed, in whom is no guile! *St. John* i 47.

To Nathanael.

Before that Philip called thee, when thou wast under the fig tree, I saw thee. *St. John* i. 48.

Nathanael. Rabbi, Thou art the Son of God.

Because I said unto thee, I saw thee under the fig tree, believest thou? thou shalt see greater things than these. Verily, verily, I say unto you, Hereafter ye shall see heaven open, and the angels of God ascending and descending upon the Son of man. *St. John* i. 50. 51.

First Miracle—at Marriage Feast.

CANA OF GALILEE.

His Mother.   They have no wine.

    Woman, what have I to do with thee? Mine hour is not yet come.   *St. John* ii. 4.

To the Servants.

    Fill the waterpots with water.
    Draw out now, and bear unto the governor of the feast.   *St. John* ii. 7, 8.

First Passover at Jerusalem.

CLEANSING OF THE TEMPLE.

April, A.D. 27.

    Take these things hence; make not My Father's house an house of merchandise.

The Jews.   What sign showest Thou?

    Destroy this temple, and in three days I will raise it up.   *St. John* ii. 16, 19.

Discourse with Nicodemus.

JERUSALEM.

    Verily, verily, I say unto thee, Except a man be born again, he cannot see the kingdom of God.

Nicodemus.   How can a man be born when he is old?

    Verily, verily, I say unto thee, Except a man be born of water and of the Spirit, he cannot enter into the kingdom of God.   That which is born of the flesh is flesh; and that which is born of the Spirit is spirit.

Marvel not that I said unto thee, Ye must be born again. The wind bloweth where it listeth, and thou hearest the sound thereof, but canst not tell whence it cometh, and whither it goeth: so is every one that is born of the Spirit.

Nicodemus. How can these things be?

Art thou a master of Israel, and knowest not these things?

Verily, verily, I say unto thee, We speak that we do know, and testify that we have seen; and ye receive not our witness. If I have told you earthly things, and ye believe not, how shall ye believe, if I tell you of heavenly things? And no man hath ascended up to heaven, but He that came down from heaven, even the Son of man which is in heaven.

And as Moses lifted up the serpent in the wilderness, even so must the Son of man be lifted up: that whosoever believeth in Him should not perish, but have eternal life. For God so loved the world, that He gave His only begotten Son, that whosoever believeth in Him should not perish, but have everlasting life. For God sent not His Son into the world to condemn the world; but that the world through Him might be saved.

He that believeth on Him is not condemned: but he that believeth not is condemned already, because he hath not believed in the Name of the only begotten Son of God. And this is the condemnation, that light is come into the world, and men loved darkness rather than light, because their deeds were evil.

For every one that doeth evil hateth the light,

neither cometh to the light, lest his deeds should be reproved. But he that doeth truth cometh to the light, that his deeds may be made manifest, that they are wrought in God. *St. John* iii. 3–21.

Discourse with Samaritan Woman.

By Jacob's Well at Sychar.

April, A.D. 27.

To the Woman.

Give Me to drink.

Woman. How is it that Thou, being a Jew, askest drink of me?

If thou knewest the gift of God, and who it is that saith to thee, Give Me to drink; thou wouldest have asked of Him, and He would have given thee living water.

Woman. From whence hast Thou that living water?

Whosoever drinketh of this water shall thirst again : but whosoever drinketh of the water that I shall give him shall never thirst; but the water that I shall give him shall be in him a well of water springing up into everlasting life.

Woman. Sir, give me this water.

Go, call thy husband, and come hither.

Woman. I have no husband.

Thou hast well said, I have no husband : for thou hast had five husbands; and he whom thou now hast is not thy husband : in that saidst thou truly.

Woman. Our fathers worshipped in this mountain.

Woman, believe Me, the hour cometh, when ye shall neither in this mountain, nor yet at Jerusalem, worship the Father. Ye worship ye know not what: we know what we worship: for salvation is of the Jews.

But the hour cometh, and now is, when the true worshippers shall worship the Father in spirit and in truth: for the Father seeketh such to worship Him. God is a Spirit: and they that worship Him must worship Him in spirit and in truth.

Woman. I know that Messias cometh, which is called Christ.

I that speak unto thee am He.   *St. John* iv. 7-26.

To the Disciples.

I have meat to eat that ye know not of.

My meat is to do the will of Him that sent Me, and to finish His work.

Say not ye, There are yet four months, and then cometh harvest? behold, I say unto you, Lift up your eyes, and look on the fields; for they are white already to harvest. And he that reapeth receiveth wages, and gathereth fruit unto life eternal: that both he that soweth and he that reapeth may rejoice together. And herein is that saying true, One soweth, and another reapeth. I sent you to reap that whereon ye bestowed no labour: other men laboured, and ye are entered into their labours.   *St. John* iv. 32-38.

Healing the Nobleman's Son.

CANA OF GALILEE.

To the Nobleman.

Except ye see signs and wonders, ye will not believe.

Nobleman. Sir, come down ere my child die.

Go thy way; thy son liveth.   *St. John* iv. 48, 50.

Healing of Impotent Man.

JERUSALEM: BY THE POOL OF BETHESDA.

February, A D. 28.

To the Impotent Man.

Wilt thou be made whole?

Impotent man.   I have no man . . . to put me into the pool.

Rise, take up thy bed, and walk.   *St. John* v. 6, 8.

IN THE TEMPLE.

To the Man made whole.

Behold, thou art made whole: sin no more, lest a worse thing come unto thee.

To the Jews.

My Father worketh hitherto, and I work.

Verily, verily, I say unto you, The Son can do nothing of Himself, but what He seeth the Father do: for what things soever He doeth, these also doeth the Son likewise. For the Father loveth the Son, and showeth Him all things that Himself doeth: and He will show Him greater works than these, that ye may marvel.

For as the Father raiseth up the dead, and quickeneth them; even so the Son quickeneth whom He will. For the Father judgeth no man, but hath committed all judgment unto the Son: that all men should honour the Son, even as they honour the Father. He that honoureth not the Son honoureth not the Father which hath sent Him.

Verily, verily, I say unto you, He that heareth My word, and believeth on Him that sent Me, hath everlasting life, and shall not come into condemnation; but is passed from death unto life. Verily, verily, I say unto you, The hour is coming, and now is, when the dead shall hear the voice of the Son of God: and they that hear shall live. For as the Father hath life in Himself; so hath He given to the Son to have life in Himself; and hath given Him authority to execute judgment also, because He is the Son of man. Marvel not at this: for the hour is coming, in the which all that are in the graves shall hear His voice, and shall come forth; they that have done good, unto the resurrection of life; and they that have done evil, unto the resurrection of damnation.

I can of Mine own self do nothing: as I hear, I judge: and My judgment is just; because I seek not Mine own will, but the will of the Father which hath sent Me. If I bear witness of Myself, My witness is not true. There is another that beareth witness of Me; and I know that the witness which He witnesseth of Me is true.

Ye sent unto John, and he bare witness unto the truth. But I receive not testimony from man: but these things I say, that ye might be saved.

He was a burning and a shining light: and ye were willing for a season to rejoice in his light. But I have greater witness than that of John: for the works which the Father hath given Me to finish, the same works that I do, bear witness of Me, that the Father hath sent Me. And the Father Himself, which hath sent Me, hath borne witness of Me. Ye have neither heard His voice at any time, nor seen His shape. And ye have not His word abiding in you: for whom He hath sent, Him ye believe not.

Search the Scriptures; for in them ye think ye

have eternal life: and they are they which testify of Me. And ye will not come to Me, that ye might have life.

I receive not honour from men. But I know you, that ye have not the love of God in you. I am come in My Father's Name, and ye receive Me not: if another shall come in his own name, him ye will receive.

How can ye believe, which receive honour one of another, and seek not the honour that cometh from God only?

Do not think that I will accuse you to the Father: there is one that accuseth you, even Moses, in whom ye trust. For had ye believed Moses, ye would have believed Me: for he wrote of Me. But if ye believe not his writings, how shall ye believe My words? *St. John* v. 14, 17, 19–47.

THIRD PERIOD.[1]

FIRST PUBLIC MINISTRY IN GALILEE.

From the departure of Jesus from Jerusalem, on learning of the Baptist's imprisonment, February, A.D. 28, *to His final departure from Galilee, October,* A.D. 28.

PART I.

From the beginning of Galilæan ministry, February, A.D. 28, *to the Mission of the Twelve Apostles, March,* A.D. 28.

[1] Divided, for greater clearness, into two parts.

JOURNEYINGS OF OUR LORD DURING THE THIRD PERIOD.

PART I.

From His leaving Jerusalem for Galilee, February, A.D. 28 (*St. Matt.* iv. 12; *St. Mark* i. 14), *to the death of St. John the Baptist, about March*, A.D. 28.

FROM JERUSALEM TO NAZARETH . . .	*St. Luke* iv. 14, 16.
TO CAPERNAUM	*St. Luke* iv. 31.
CIRCUIT THROUGH GALILÆAN TOWNS . . .	*St. Mark* i. 38, 39.
RETURN TO CAPERNAUM	*St. Mark* ii. 1.
THE MOUNTAIN OF THE GREAT SERMON: HILL ABOVE GENNESARET	*St. Matt.* v. 1.
RETURN TO CAPERNAUM . . .	*St. Luke* vii. 1.
TO NAIN	*St. Luke* vii. 11.
SECOND CIRCUIT IN GALILEE	*St. Luke* viii. 1.
ACROSS THE LAKE OF GENNESARET TO THE COUNTRY OF THE GADARENES . . . . *St. Luke* viii. 22, 26;	*St. Mark* v. 1.
RETURN TO CAPERNAUM . . .	*St. Mark* v. 21.
TO NAZARETH	*St. Mark* vi. 1.
THROUGH THE VILLAGES AROUND	*St. Mark* vi. 6.
RETURN (PROBABLY) TO CAPERNAUM FOR MISSION OF THE TWELVE	*St. Mark* vi. 7.

CHIEF EVENTS RECORDED IN THE THIRD PERIOD.

PART I.

OUR LORD REJECTED AT NAZARETH . .	*St. Luke* iv. 28-31.
MIRACULOUS DRAUGHT OF FISHES	*St. Luke* v. 1-11.
SECOND CALL OF PETER AND ANDREW, JAMES AND JOHN	*St. Matt.* iv. 18-22.

A Devil cast out at Capernaum . . . *St. Mark* i. 23-28.
Peter's Mother-in-law healed, and many others
             St. Mark i. 29-34.
First Galilæan Tour . . . . *St. Mark* i. 35-39.
Sermon on the Mount . . . . . . *St. Matt.* v., vi., vii.
Healing of the Leper . . . . *St. Matt.* viii. 1-4.
Paralytic Man absolved and healed . . *St. Matt.* ix. 1-8.
Call of Levi . . . . *St. Matt.* ix. 9-13.
Pharisees offended at Disciples plucking Corn on the
 Sabbath . . . . *St. Matt.* xii. 1-8.
The Withered Hand healed . . . . *St. Matt.* xii. 9-13.
First Council held against Jesus . . *St. Matt.* xii. 14-21.
Great Mulitudes following Him . . . *St. Mark* iii. 6-12.
Twelve Apostles chosen . . . . . *St. Luke* vi. 13-19.
Centurion's Servant healed . . . . *St. Luke* vii. 1-10.
Raising of the Widow's Son at Nain . . *St. Luke* vii. 11-17.
Message from the Baptist, and Answer . *St. Luke* vii. 18-35.
Feast at House of Simon the Pharisee . *St. Luke* vii. 36-50.
Second Galilæan Tour . . . . . . *St. Luke* viii. 1-3.
The Parables of the Kingdom . . . . . *St. Matt.* xiii.
Healing of a Demoniac at Capernaum . *St. Matt.* xii. 22-45.
His Mother and Brethren seek Him . . *St. Matt.* xii. 46-50.
Calming of the Storm on the Lake . . *St. Matt.* viii. 18-27.
Healing of the Gadarene Demoniacs . . *St. Matt.* viii. 28-34
The Woman with Issue of Blood healed . *St. Matt.* ix. 20-22
Raising of Jairus's Daughter . . . *St. Matt.* ix. 18, 19, 23-26.
Two Blind Men healed, and a Devil cast out
             St. Matt. ix. 27-34.
A Second Time rejected at Nazareth
       St. Mark vi. 1-6; *St. Matt.* xiii. 54-58.
Third Galilæan Tour . . . . . *St. Matt.* ix. 35.
Mission of the Twelve . . . . . *St. Matt.* x. 1-42.
Death of St. John the Baptist . . . . *St. Matt.* xiv. 1-12

First Public Ministry.

Galilee.

A.D. 28.

The time is fulfilled, and the kingdom of God is at hand: repent ye, and believe the gospel.

St. Mark i. 15.
(Cf. *St. Matt.* iv. 17.)

The Synagogue at Nazareth.

"The Spirit of the Lord is upon Me, because He hath anointed Me to preach the gospel to the poor; He hath sent Me to heal the brokenhearted, to preach deliverance to the captives, and recovering of sight to the blind, to set at liberty them that are bruised, to preach the acceptable year of the Lord." *St. Luke* iv. 18, 19.

This day is this Scripture fulfilled in your ears.

Ye will surely say unto Me this proverb, Physician, heal Thyself: whatsoever we have heard done in Capernaum, do also here in Thy country.

Verily I say unto you, No prophet is accepted in his own country. But I tell you of a truth, many widows were in Israel in the days of Elias,

when the heaven was shut up three years and six months, when great famine was throughout all the land; but unto none of them was Elias sent, save unto Sarepta, a city of Sidon, unto a woman that was a widow. And many lepers were in Israel in the time of Eliseus the prophet; and none of them was cleansed, saving Naaman the Syrian.
St. Luke iv. 21-27.

Second Call of Andrew and Peter, James and John.
BY THE SEA OF GALILEE.

Come ye after Me, and I will make you to become fishers of men. *St. Mark* i. 17.
(Cf. *St. Matt.* iv. 19.)

Casting out a Devil.
CAPERNAUM.

Hold thy peace, and come out of him.
St. Mark i. 25.
(Cf. *St. Luke* iv. 35.)

Before First Circuit in Galilee.
CAPERNAUM.

The disciples. All men seek for Thee.

Let us go into the next towns, that I may preach there also: for therefore came I forth.
St. Mark i. 38.
(Cf. *St. Luke* iv. 43.)

Miraculous Draught of Fishes.
By the Lake of Gennesaret.

To St. Peter.

Launch out into the deep, and let down your nets for a draught.

Peter.   *Depart from me; for I am a sinful man, O Lord.*

Fear not; from henceforth thou shalt catch men.

St. Luke v. 4, 10.

The Sermon on the Mount.
Hill above Gennesaret.

Blessed are the poor in spirit: for theirs is the kingdom of heaven.

Blessed are they that mourn: for they shall be comforted.

Blessed are the meek: for they shall inherit the earth.

Blessed are they which do hunger and thirst after righteousness: for they shall be filled.

Blessed are the merciful: for they shall obtain mercy.

Blessed are the pure in heart: for they shall see God.

Blessed are the peacemakers: for they shall be called the children of God.

Blessed are they which are persecuted for righteousness' sake: for theirs is the kingdom of heaven.

Blessed are ye, when men shall revile you, and persecute you, and shall say all manner of evil against you falsely, for My sake. Rejoice, and be exceeding glad: for great is your reward in heaven: for so persecuted they the prophets which were before you.

Ye are the salt of the earth: but if the salt have lost his savour, wherewith shall it be salted? it is thenceforth good for nothing, but to be cast out, and to be trodden under foot of men.

Ye are the light of the world. A city that is set on an hill cannot be hid. Neither do men light a candle, and put it under a bushel, but on a candlestick; and it giveth light unto all that are in the house. Let your light so shine before men, that they may see your good works, and glorify your Father which is in heaven.

Think not that I am come to destroy the law, or the prophets: I am not come to destroy, but to fulfil. For verily I say unto you, Till heaven and earth pass, one jot or one tittle shall in no wise pass from the law, till all be fulfilled. Whosoever therefore shall break one of these least commandments, and shall teach men so, he shall be called the least in the kingdom of heaven: but whosoever shall do and teach them, the same shall be called great in the kingdom of heaven. For I say unto you, That except your righteousness shall exceed the righteousness of the scribes and Pharisees, ye shall in no case enter into the kingdom of heaven.

Ye have heard that it was said by them of old time, Thou shalt not kill; and whosoever shall kill shall be in danger of the judgment: but I say unto you, That whosoever is angry with his brother without a cause shall be in danger of the judgment: and whosoever shall say to his brother, Raca, shall be in danger of the council: but whosoever shall say, Thou fool, shall be in danger of hell fire.

Therefore if thou bring thy gift to the altar, and there rememberest that thy brother hath aught against thee; leave there thy gift before the altar, and go thy way; first be reconciled to thy brother, and then come and offer thy gift.

Agree with thine adversary quickly, whiles thou art in the way with him; lest at any time the adversary deliver thee to the judge, and the judge deliver thee to the officer, and thou be cast into prison. Verily I say unto thee, Thou shalt by no means come out thence, till thou hast paid the uttermost farthing.

Ye have heard that it was said by them of old time, Thou shalt not commit adultery: but I say unto you, That whosoever looketh on a woman to lust after her hath committed adultery with her already in his heart.

And if thy right eye offend thee, pluck it out, and cast it from thee: for it is profitable for thee that one of thy members should perish, and not that thy whole body should be cast into hell. And if thy right hand offend thee, cut it off, and cast it from thee: for it is profitable for thee that one of thy members should perish, and not that thy whole body should be cast into hell.

It hath been said, Whosoever shall put away his wife, let him give her a writing of divorcement: but I say unto you, That whosoever shall put away his wife, saving for the cause of fornication, causeth her to commit adultery: and whosoever shall marry her that is divorced committeth adultery.

Again, ye have heard that it hath been said by

them of old time, Thou shalt not forswear thyself, but shalt perform unto the Lord thine oaths: but I say unto you, Swear not at all; neither by heaven; for it is God's throne: nor by the earth; for it is His footstool: neither by Jerusalem; for it is the city of the great King. Neither shalt thou swear by thy head, because thou canst not make one hair white or black. But let your communication be, Yea, yea; Nay, nay: for whatsoever is more than these cometh of evil.

Ye have heard that it hath been said, An eye for an eye, and a tooth for a tooth: but I say unto you, That ye resist not evil: but whosoever shall smite thee on thy right cheek, turn to him the other also. And if any man will sue thee at the law, and take away thy coat, let him have thy cloke also. And whosoever shall compel thee to go a mile, go with him twain.

Give to him that asketh thee, and from him that would borrow of thee turn not thou away.

Ye have heard that it hath been said, Thou shalt love thy neighbour, and hate thine enemy. But I say unto you, Love your enemies, bless them that curse you, do good to them that hate you, and pray for them which despitefully use you, and persecute you; that ye may be the children of your Father which is in heaven: for He maketh His sun to rise on the evil and on the good, and sendeth rain on the just and on the unjust.

For if ye love them which love you, what reward have ye? do not even the publicans the same? And if ye salute your brethren only, what do ye more than others? do not even the publicans so? Be ye therefore perfect, even as your Father which is in heaven is perfect.

Take heed that ye do not your alms before men, to be seen of them: otherwise ye have no reward of your Father which is in heaven. Therefore when thou doest thine alms, do not sound a trumpet before thee, as the hypocrites do in the synagogues and in the streets, that they may have glory of men. Verily I say unto you, They have their reward. But when thou doest alms, let not thy left hand know what thy right hand doeth: that thine alms may be in secret: and thy Father, which seeth in secret, Himself shall reward thee openly.

And when thou prayest, thou shalt not be as the hypocrites are: for they love to pray standing in the synagogues and in the corners of the streets, that they may be seen of men. Verily I say unto you, They have their reward. But thou, when thou prayest, enter into thy closet, and when thou hast shut thy door, pray to thy Father which is in secret; and thy Father, which seeth in secret, shall reward thee openly.

But when ye pray, use not vain repetitions, as the heathen do: for they think that they shall be heard for their much speaking. Be not ye therefore like unto them: for your Father knoweth what things ye have need of, before ye ask Him.

After this manner therefore pray ye: Our Father which art in heaven, Hallowed be Thy Name. Thy kingdom come. Thy will be done in earth, as it is in heaven. Give us this day our daily bread. And forgive us our debts, as we forgive our debtors. And lead us not into temptation, but deliver us from evil: For Thine is the kingdom, and the power, and the glory, for ever. Amen.

For if ye forgive men their trespasses, your heavenly Father will also forgive you: but if ye forgive not men their trespasses, neither will your Father forgive your trespasses.

Moreover when ye fast, be not, as the hypocrites, of a sad countenance: for they disfigure their faces, that they may appear unto men to fast. Verily I say unto you, They have their reward. But thou, when thou fastest, anoint thine head, and wash thy face; that thou appear not unto men to fast, but unto thy Father which is in secret: and thy Father, which seeth in secret, shall reward thee openly.

Lay not up for yourselves treasures upon earth, where moth and rust doth corrupt, and where thieves break through and steal: but lay up for yourselves treasures in heaven, where neither moth nor rust doth corrupt, and where thieves do not break through nor steal: for where your treasure is, there will your heart be also.

The light of the body is the eye: if therefore thine eye be single, thy whole body shall be full of light. But if thine eye be evil, thy whole body shall be full of darkness. If therefore the light that is in thee be darkness, how great is that darkness!

No man can serve two masters: for either he will hate the one, and love the other; or else he will hold to the one, and despise the other. Ye cannot serve God and mammon.

Therefore I say unto you, Take no thought for your life, what ye shall eat, or what ye shall drink; nor yet for your body, what ye shall put on. Is not the life more than meat, and the body than raiment? Behold the fowls of the air: for they sow not, neither do they reap, nor gather into barns; yet your heavenly Father feedeth them. Are ye not much better than they?

Which of you by taking thought can add one cubit unto his stature? And why take ye thought for raiment? Consider the lilies of the field, how they grow; they toil not, neither do they spin: and yet I say unto you, That even Solomon in all his glory was not arrayed like one of these.

Wherefore, if God so clothe the grass of the field, which to-day is, and to-morrow is cast into the oven, shall He not much more clothe you, O ye of little faith?

Therefore take no thought, saying, What shall we eat? or, What shall we drink? or, Wherewithal shall we be clothed? (For after all these things do the Gentiles seek:) for your heavenly Father knoweth that ye have need of all these things. But seek ye first the kingdom of God, and His righteousness; and all these things shall be added unto you.

Take therefore no thought for the morrow: for the morrow shall take thought for the things of itself. Sufficient unto the day is the evil thereof.

Judge not, that ye be not judged. For with what judgment ye judge, ye shall be judged: and with what measure ye mete, it shall be measured to you again.

And why beholdest thou the mote that is in thy brother's eye, but considerest not the beam that is in thine own eye? Or how wilt thou say to thy brother, Let me pull out the mote out of thine eye; and, behold, a beam is in thine own eye? Thou hypocrite, first cast out the beam out of thine own eye; and then shalt thou see clearly to cast out the mote out of thy brother's eye.

Give not that which is holy unto the dogs, neither cast ye your pearls before swine, lest they trample them under their feet, and turn again and rend you.

Ask, and it shall be given you; seek, and ye shall find; knock, and it shall be opened unto you: for every one that asketh receiveth; and he that seeketh findeth; and to him that knocketh it shall be opened.

Or what man is there of you, whom if his son ask bread, will he give him a stone? or if he ask a fish, will he give him a serpent?

If ye then, being evil, know how to give good gifts unto your children, how much more shall your Father which is in heaven give good things to them that ask Him? Therefore all things whatsoever ye would that men should do to you, do ye even so to them: for this is the law and the prophets.

Enter ye in at the strait gate; for wide is the gate, and broad is the way, that leadeth to destruction, and many there be which go in thereat: because strait is the gate, and narrow is the way, which leadeth unto life, and few there be that find it.

Beware of false prophets, which come to you in sheep's clothing, but inwardly they are ravening wolves. Ye shall know them by their fruits. Do men gather grapes of thorns, or figs of thistles?

Even so every good tree bringeth forth good fruit; but a corrupt tree bringeth forth evil fruit. A good tree cannot bring forth evil fruit, neither can a corrupt tree bring forth good fruit. Every tree that bringeth not forth good fruit is hewn down, and cast into the fire. Wherefore by their fruits ye shall know them.

Not every one that saith unto Me, Lord, Lord, shall enter into the kingdom of heaven; but he that doeth the will of My Father which is in heaven. Many will say to Me in that day, Lord, Lord, have we not prophesied in Thy Name? and in Thy Name have cast out devils? and in Thy Name done many wonderful works? And then will I profess unto them, I never knew you: depart from Me, ye that work iniquity.

Therefore whosoever heareth these sayings of Mine, and doeth them, I will liken him unto a wise man, which built his house upon a rock: and the rain descended, and the floods came, and the winds blew, and beat upon that house; and it fell not: for it was founded upon a rock.

And every one that heareth these sayings of Mine, and doeth them not, shall be likened unto a foolish man, which built his house upon the sand: and the rain descended, and the floods came, and the winds blew, and beat upon that house; and it fell: and great was the fall of it. *St. Matt.* v., vi., vii.
(Cf. *St. Luke* vi. 20–49.)

Healing of the Leper.

Leper. *If Thou wilt, Thou canst make me clean.*

I will; be thou clean.

See thou say nothing to any man: but go thy way, shew thyself to the priest, and offer for thy cleansing those things which Moses commanded, for a testimony unto them. *St. Mark* i. 41, 44.
(Cf. *St. Matt.* viii. 3, 4; *St. Luke* v. 13, 14.)

Healing of Paralytic Man, borne of Four.

CAPERNAUM.

To the Sick Man.

Son, be of good cheer; thy sins be forgiven thee.

To the Scribes.

Wherefore think ye evil in your hearts? For whether is easier, to say, Thy sins be forgiven thee; or to say, Arise, and walk? But that ye may know that the Son of man hath power on earth to forgive sins,

To the Sick Man.

Arise, take up thy bed, and go unto thine house.
St. Matt. ix. 2, 4-6.

(Cf. *St. Mark* ii. 5, 8-11; *St. Luke* v. 20, 22-24.)

Call of St. Matthew (Levi).

CAPERNAUM.

Follow Me. *St. Matt.* ix. 9.

(Cf. *St. Mark* ii. 14; *St. Luke* v. 27.)

AT THE FEAST IN LEVI'S HOUSE.

They that be whole need not a physician, but they that are sick. But go ye and learn what that meaneth, I will have mercy, and not sacrifice: for I am not come to call the righteous, but sinners to repentance. *St. Matt.* ix. 12, 13.

(Cf. *St. Mark* ii. 17; *St. Luke* v. 31, 32.)

On Fasting.
CAPERNAUM.

Disciples of John. Thy disciples fast not.

Can the children of the bridechamber fast, while the bridegroom is with them? as long as they have the bridegroom with them, they cannot fast. But the days will come, when the bridegroom shall be taken away from them, and then shall they fast in those days.   *St. Mark* ii. 19, 20.
(Cf. *St. Matt.* ix. 15; *St. Luke* v. 34, 35.)

Parable of New Cloth and New Wine.

No man putteth a piece of a new garment upon an old; if otherwise, then both the new maketh a rent, and the piece that was taken out of the new agreeth not with the old.

And no man putteth new wine into old bottles; else the new wine will burst the bottles, and be spilled, and the bottles shall perish. But new wine must be put into new bottles; and both are preserved.

No man also having drunk old wine straightway desireth new: for he saith, The old is better.
St. Luke v. 36-39.
(Cf. *St. Matt.* ix. 16, 17; *St. Mark* ii. 21, 22.)

Disciples plucking Ears of Corn on the Sabbath.
GALILEE.

Pharisees. Thy disciples do that which is not lawful to do on the sabbath day.

To the Pharisees.
Have ye not read so much as this, what David

did, when himself was an hungred, and they which were with him;[1] how he went into the house of God in the days of Abiathar the high priest, and did eat the shewbread, which is not lawful to eat but for the priests, and gave also to them which were with him?[2]

[1] *St. Luke* vi. 3; [2] *St. Mark* ii. 26.

Or have ye not read in the Law, how that on the sabbath days the priests in the temple profane the sabbath, and are blameless? But I say unto you, That in this place is One greater than the temple.

But if ye had known what this meaneth, I will have mercy, and not sacrifice, ye would not have condemned the guiltless. *St. Matt.* xii. 5–7.

The sabbath was made for man, and not man for the sabbath: therefore the Son of man is Lord also of the sabbath. *St. Mark* ii. 27, 28.

The Withered Hand healed on the Sabbath.

SYNAGOGUE OF CAPERNAUM.

Scribes and Pharisees. Is it lawful to heal on the sabbath day?

To the Man with the Withered Hand.

Rise up, and stand forth in the midst.

To the Scribes and Pharisees.

I will ask you one thing; Is it lawful on the sabbath days to do good, or to do evil? to save life, or to destroy it? *St. Luke* vi. 8, 9.

What man shall there be among you, that shall have one sheep, and if it fall into a pit on the sabbath day, will he not lay hold on it, and lift it out? How much then is a man better than a sheep? Wherefore it is lawful to do well on the sabbath days.

To the Man.

Stretch forth thine hand. *St. Matt.* xii. 11-13.

Centurion's Servant healed.
CAPERNAUM.

To the Centurion.

I will come and heal him. *St. Matt.* viii. 7.

Centurion. Lord, I am not worthy that Thou shouldest come under my roof.

To the People that followed.

Verily I say unto you, I have not found so great faith, no, not in Israel. And I say unto you, That many shall come from the east and west, and shall sit down with Abraham, and Isaac, and Jacob, in the kingdom of heaven. But the children of the kingdom shall be cast out into outer darkness: there shall be weeping and gnashing of teeth.

To the Centurion.

Go thy way; and as thou hast believed, so be it done unto thee. *St. Matt.* viii. 10-13.

(Cf. *St. Luke* vii. 1-10.)

Raising of the Widow's Son.
NAIN.

To the Mother.

Weep not.

To him that was dead.

Young man, I say unto thee, Arise.
St. Luke vii. 13, 14.

St. John the Baptist's Message.
CAPERNAUM.

St. John's two disciples. Art Thou He that should come?

Go your way, and tell John what things ye have seen and heard; how that the blind see, the lame walk, the lepers are cleansed, the deaf hear, the dead are raised, to the poor the gospel is preached. And blessed is he, whosoever shall not be offended in Me.
St. Luke vii. 22, 23.
(Cf. *St. Matt.* xi. 4–6.)

To the People concerning John.

What went ye out into the wilderness for to see? A reed shaken with the wind? But what went ye out for to see? A man clothed in soft raiment? Behold, they which are gorgeously apparelled, and live delicately, are in kings' courts. But what went ye out for to see? A prophet? Yea, I say unto you, and much more than a prophet. This is he, of whom it is written, Behold, I send My messenger before Thy face, which shall prepare Thy way before Thee.
St. Luke vii. 24–27.

Verily I say unto you, Among them that are born of women there hath not risen a greater than John the Baptist: notwithstanding he that is least in the kingdom of heaven is greater than he.

And from the days of John the Baptist until now the kingdom of heaven suffereth violence, and the violent take it by force.

For all the prophets and the Law prophesied until John.

And if ye will receive it, this is Elias, which was for to come.

He that hath ears to hear, let him hear.

But whereunto shall I liken this generation? It is like unto children sitting in the markets, and calling unto their fellows, and saying, We have piped unto you, and ye have not danced; we have mourned unto you, and ye have not lamented.

For John came neither eating nor drinking, and they say, He hath a devil. The Son of man came eating and drinking, and they say, Behold a man gluttonous, and a winebibber, a friend of publicans and sinners. But wisdom is justified of her children. *St. Matt.* xi. 11–19.
(Cf. *St. Luke* vii. 27–35.)

Mary Magdalene washing His Feet.

CAPERNAUM: IN THE HOUSE OF SIMON THE PHARISEE.

To Simon.

Simon, I have somewhat to say unto thee. There was a certain creditor which had two debtors: the one owed five hundred pence, and the other fifty. And when they had nothing to pay, he frankly forgave them both. Tell me therefore, which of them will love him most?

Simon. He to whom he forgave most.

Thou hast rightly judged. Seest thou this woman? I entered into thine house, thou gavest Me no water for My feet: but she hath washed My feet with tears, and wiped them with the hairs of her head. Thou gavest Me no kiss: but this woman since the time I came in hath not ceased to kiss My feet. My head with oil thou didst not anoint: but this woman hath anointed My feet with ointment.

Wherefore I say unto thee, Her sins, which are many, are forgiven; for she loved much: but to whom little is given, the same loveth little.

To the Magdalene.

Thy sins are forgiven. Thy faith hath saved thee; go in peace. *St. Luke* vii. 40-48, 50.

Five Parables spoken to the Multitude.
PLAIN OF GENNESARET.

1. The Sower.

Hearken; Behold, there went out a sower to sow: and it came to pass, as he sowed, some fell by the way side, and the fowls of the air came and devoured it up.

And some fell on stony ground, where it had not much earth; and immediately it sprang up, because it had no depth of earth: but when the sun was up, it was scorched; and because it had no root, it withered away.

And some fell among thorns, and the thorns grew up, and choked it, and it yielded no fruit.

And other fell on good ground, and did yield fruit that sprang up and increased; and brought forth, some thirty, and some sixty, and some an hundred. He that hath ears to hear, let him hear.

St. Mark iv. 3-9.
(Cf. *St. Matt.* xiii. 3-9; *St. Luke* viii. 5-8.)

2. Gradual ripening of Corn.

So is the kingdom of God, as if a man should cast seed into the ground; and should sleep, and rise night and day, and the seed should spring and grow up, he knoweth not how.

For the earth bringeth forth fruit of herself; first the blade, then the ear, after that the full corn in the ear. But when the fruit is brought forth, immediately he putteth in the sickle, because the harvest is come. *St. Mark* iv. 26–29.

3. The Tares.

The kingdom of heaven is likened unto a man which sowed good seed in his field: but while men slept, his enemy came and sowed tares among the wheat, and went his way. But when the blade was sprung up, and brought forth fruit, then appeared the tares also.

So the servants of the householder came and said unto him, Sir, didst not thou sow good seed in thy field? from whence then hath it tares? He said unto them, An enemy hath done this. The servants said unto him, Wilt thou then that we go and gather them up? But he said, Nay; lest while ye gather up the tares, ye root up also the wheat with them. Let both grow together until the harvest: and in the time of harvest I will say to the reapers, Gather ye together first the tares, and bind them in bundles to burn them: but gather the wheat into my barn. *St. Matt.* xiii. 24–30.

4. The Mustard Seed.

Whereunto shall we liken the kingdom of God? or with what comparison shall we compare it? It

is like a grain of mustard seed, which, when it is sown in the earth, is less than all the seeds that be in the earth: but when it is sown, it groweth up, and becometh greater than all herbs, and shooteth out great branches; so that the fowls of the air may lodge under the shadow of it.
St. Mark iv. 30–32.
(Cf. *St. Matt.* xiii. 31, 32; *St. Luke* xiii. 18, 19.)

5. The Leaven.

Whereunto shall I liken the kingdom of God? It is like leaven, which a woman took and hid in three measures of meal, till the whole was leavened. *St. Luke* xiii. 20, 21.
(Cf. *St. Matt.* xiii. 33.)

Parables explained.

In the House with His Disciples.

Disciples. Why speakest Thou unto them in parables?
Unto you it is given to know the mystery of the kingdom of God: but unto them that are without, all these things are done in parables. *St. Mark* iv. 11.

For whosoever hath, to him shall be given, and he shall have more abundance: but whosoever hath not, from him shall be taken away even that he hath. *St. Matt.* xiii. 12.

Therefore speak I to them in parables: that seeing they may see, and not perceive; and hearing they may hear, and not understand; lest at any time they should be converted, and their sins should be forgiven them. *St. Mark* iv. 12.

And in them is fulfilled the prophecy of Esaias,

which saith, By hearing ye shall hear, and shall not understand; and seeing ye shall see, and shall not perceive: for this people's heart is waxed gross, and their ears are dull of hearing, and their eyes they have closed; lest at any time they should see with their eyes, and hear with their ears, and should understand with their heart, and should be converted, and I should heal them.

But blessed are your eyes, for they see: and your ears, for they hear. For verily I say unto you, That many prophets and righteous men have desired to see those things which ye see, and have not seen them; and to hear those things which ye hear, and have not heard them. *St. Matt.* xiii. 14-17.

Know ye not this parable? and how then will ye know all parables? *St. Mark* iv. 13.

Hear ye therefore the parable of the sower.

When any one heareth the word of the kingdom, and understandeth it not, then cometh the wicked one, and catcheth away that which was sown in his heart. This is he which received seed by the way side.

But he that received the seed into stony places, the same is he that heareth the word, and anon with joy receiveth it; yet hath he not root in himself, but dureth for a while: for when tribulation or persecution ariseth because of the word, by and by he is offended.

He also that received seed among the thorns is he that heareth the word; and the care of this world, and the deceitfulness of riches,[1] and the lusts of other things entering in, choke the word, and it becometh unfruitful.[2]

[1] *St. Matt.* xiii. 18-22; [2] *St. Mark* iv. 19.

But he that received seed into the good

ground is he that heareth the word, and understandeth it; which also beareth fruit, and bringeth forth, some an hundredfold, some sixty, some thirty. *St. Matt.* xiii. 23.

(Cf. *St. Mark* iv. 11–15; *St. Luke* viii. 9–15.)

Is a candle brought to be put under a bushel, or under a bed? and not to be set on a candlestick? For there is nothing hid, which shall not be manifested; neither was any thing kept secret, but that it should come abroad. If any man have ears to hear, let him hear.

Take heed what ye hear: with what measure ye mete, it shall be measured to you: and unto you that hear shall more be given. For he that hath, to him shall be given: and he that hath not, from him shall be taken even that which he hath.

St. Mark iv. 21–25.

(Cf. *St. Luke* viii. 16–18.)

The disciples. Declare unto us the parable of the tares.

He that soweth the good seed is the Son of man; the field is the world; the good seed are the children of the kingdom; but the tares are the children of the wicked one; the enemy that sowed them is the devil; the harvest is the end of the world; and the reapers are the angels.

As therefore the tares are gathered and burned in the fire; so shall it be in the end of this world.

The Son of man shall send forth His angels, and they shall gather out of His kingdom all things that offend, and them which do iniquity; and shall cast them into a furnace of fire: there shall be wailing and gnashing of teeth.

Then shall the righteous shine forth as the sun in the kingdom of their Father. Who hath ears to hear, let him hear. *St. Matt.* xiii. 37–43.

Three Parables to the Disciples.

1. The Hidden Treasure.

Again, the kingdom of heaven is like unto treasure hid in a field; the which when a man hath found, he hideth, and for joy thereof goeth and selleth all that he hath, and buyeth that field.

2. The Pearl.

Again, the kingdom of heaven is like unto a merchant man, seeking goodly pearls: who, when he had found one pearl of great price, went and sold all that he had, and bought it.

3. The Net.

Again, the kingdom of heaven is like unto a net, that was cast into the sea, and gathered of every kind: which, when it was full, they drew to shore, and sat down, and gathered the good into vessels, but cast the bad away.

So shall it be at the end of the world: the angels shall come forth, and sever the wicked from amongst the just, and shall cast them into the furnace of fire: there shall be wailing and gnashing of teeth.

Have ye understood all these things?

The disciples. Yea, Lord.

Therefore every scribe which is instructed unto the kingdom of heaven is like unto a man that is an householder, which bringeth forth out of his treasure things new and old.   *St. Matt.* xiii. 44–52.

Healing of a Demoniac.

CAPERNAUM.

Every kingdom divided against itself is brought to desolation; and every city or house divided against itself shall not stand: and if Satan cast out Satan, he is divided against himself; how shall then his kingdom stand? *St. Matt.* xii. 25, 26.

And if I by Beelzebub cast out devils, by whom do your sons cast them out? therefore shall they be your judges. But if I with the finger of God cast out devils, no doubt the kingdom of God is come upon you.

When a strong man armed keepeth his palace, his goods are in peace. But when a stronger than he shall come upon him, and overcome him, he taketh from him all his armour wherein he trusted, and divideth his spoils. *St. Luke* xi. 19-22.

He that is not with Me is against Me; and he that gathereth not with Me scattereth abroad.

Wherefore I say unto you, All manner of sin and blasphemy shall be forgiven unto men: but the blasphemy against the Holy Ghost shall not be forgiven unto men. And whosoever speaketh a word against the Son of man, it shall be forgiven him: but whosoever speaketh against the Holy Ghost, it shall not be forgiven him, neither in this world, neither in the world to come.

Either make the tree good, and his fruit good; or else make the tree corrupt, and his fruit corrupt: for the tree is known by his fruit.

O generation of vipers, how can ye, being evil, speak good things? for out of the abundance of the heart the mouth speaketh. A good man out of the good treasure of the heart bringeth forth good things: and an evil man out of the evil treasure bringeth forth evil things.

But I say unto you, That every idle word that men shall speak, they shall give account thereof in the day of judgment. For by thy words thou shalt be justified, and by thy words thou shalt be condemned. *St. Matt.* xii. 30-37.

(Cf. *St. Mark* iii. 23-29; *St. Luke* xi. 17, 18, 23.)

A Sign asked for.
CAPERNAUM.

Pharisees. Master, we would see a sign from Thee.

An evil and adulterous generation seeketh after a sign; and there shall no sign be given to it, but the sign of the prophet Jonas: for as Jonas was three days and three nights in the whale's belly; so shall the Son of man be three days and three nights in the heart of the earth.

The men of Nineveh shall rise in judgment with this generation, and shall condemn it: because they repented at the preaching of Jonas; and, behold, a greater than Jonas is here. The queen of the south shall rise up in the judgment with this generation, and shall condemn it: for she came from the uttermost parts of the earth to hear the wisdom of Solomon; and, behold, a greater than Solomon is here. *St. Matt.* xii. 38-42.

(Cf. *St. Luke* xi. 29-32.)

No man, when he hath lighted a candle, putteth it in a secret place, neither under a bushel, but on a candlestick, that they which come in may see the light.

The light of the body is the eye: therefore when

thine eye is single, thy whole body also is full of light; but when thine eye is evil, thy body also is full of darkness. Take heed therefore that the light which is in thee be not darkness. If thy whole body therefore be full of light, having no part dark, the whole shall be full of light, as when the bright shining of a candle doth give thee light. *St. Luke* xi. 33-36.

The Unclean Spirit.

When the unclean spirit is gone out of a man, he walketh through dry places, seeking rest, and findeth none. Then he saith, I will return into my house from whence I came out; and when he is come, he findeth it empty, swept, and garnished. Then goeth he, and taketh with himself seven other spirits more wicked than himself, and they enter in and dwell there: and the last state of that man is worst than the first. Even so shall it be also unto this wicked generation. *St. Matt.* xii. 43-45. (Cf. *St. Luke* xi. 24-26.)

His Mother and Brethren come to Him.

CAPERNAUM.

(*His Mother sends to Him, calling Him.*)

Woman of the company. Blessed is the womb that bare Thee.

Yea rather, blessed are they that hear the word of God, and keep it. *St. Luke* xi. 27, 28

One of the crowd. Behold, Thy Mother and Thy brethren stand without.

Who is My mother? and who are My brethren? Behold My mother and My brethren! For whosoever shall do the will of My Father which is in heaven, the same is My brother, and sister, and mother.
St. Matt. xii. 48–50.

(Cf. St. Mark iii. 33–35; St. Luke viii. 21.)

Treatment of Different Followers.

To the Disciples.

Let us go over unto the other side of the lake.
St. Luke viii. 22.

A scribe. Lord, I will follow Thee.

Foxes have holes, and birds of the air have nests; but the Son of man hath not where to lay His head.

To Another.

Follow Me. St. Luke ix. 57, 58.

Suffer me first to go and bury my father.

Follow Me: and let the dead bury their dead:[1] but go thou and preach the kingdom of God.[2]

[1] St. Matt. viii. 22; [2] St. Luke ix. 60.

Another. Lord, I will follow Thee; but let me first go bid them farewell, which are at home.

No man, having put his hand to the plough, and looking back, is fit for the kingdom of God.
St. Luke ix. 61, 62.

(Cf. St. Matt. viii. 19–22.)

The Tempest on the Lake stilled.

Disciples. Lord, save us: we perish.

To the Winds and Sea.
Peace, be still.

To the Disciples.
Why are ye so fearful? how is it that ye have no faith? *St. Mark* iv. 39, 40.
(Cf. *St. Matt.* viii. 26; *St. Luke* viii. 25.)

The Demoniac among the Gadarenes.
GADARA.

Come out of the man, thou unclean spirit.

Demoniac. Torment me not.

What is thy name? *St. Mark* v. 8, 9.

Demoniac. My name is Legion.
The devils. Send us into the swine.

Go. *St. Matt.* viii. 32.

To the Man that had been possessed.
Go home to thy friends, and tell them how great things the Lord hath done for thee, and hath had compassion on thee. *St. Mark* v. 19.

The Woman with an Issue of Blood.
GENNESARET.

The woman. If I may but touch His garment, I shall be whole.

Who touched My clothes? *St. Mark* v. 30.

Peter. *The multitude throng Thee.*

Somebody hath touched Me: for I perceive that virtue is gone out of Me. *St. Luke* viii. 46.

To the Woman.
(*She told Him all the truth.*)

Daughter, be of good comfort: thy faith hath made thee whole; go in peace,[1] and be whole of thy plague.[2]   [1] *St. Luke* viii. 48; [2] *St. Mark* v. 34.
(Cf. *St. Matt.* ix. 22.)

Raising of Jairus's Daughter.

CAPERNAUM.

To Jairus.

Fear not: believe only, and she shall be made whole. *St. Luke* viii. 50.
(Cf. *St. Mark* v. 36.)

To the Mourners.

Give place. *St. Matt.* ix. 24.
Why make ye this ado, and weep? the damsel is not dead, but sleepeth. *St. Mark* v. 39.
(Cf. *St. Luke* viii. 52.)

To the Damsel.

Talitha cumi. *St. Mark* v. 41.
(Cf. *St. Luke* viii. 54.)

Two Blind Men healed.

IN THE HOUSE AT CAPERNAUM.

The blind men. *Thou Son of David, have mercy on us.*

Believe ye that I am able to do this?

Blind men.   *Yea, Lord.*

According to your faith be it unto you.
(*Their eyes opened.*)
See that no man know it.   *St. Matt.* ix. 27-30.

His Countrymen offended in Him.

NAZARETH.

A prophet is not without honour, but in his own country, and among his own kin, and in his own house.   *St. Mark* vi. 4.
(Cf. *St. Matt.* xiii. 57.)

Healing every Sickness and every Disease during the Third General Circuit.

To the Disciples.

The harvest truly is plenteous, but the labourers are few; pray ye therefore the Lord of the harvest, that He will send forth labourers into His harvest.
St. Matt. ix. 37, 38.

Mission of the Twelve Apostles.

Go not into the way of the Gentiles, and into any city of the Samaritans enter ye not: but go rather to the lost sheep of the house of Israel. And as ye go, preach, saying, The kingdom of heaven is at hand. Heal the sick, cleanse the lepers, raise the dead, cast out devils: freely ye have received, freely give.

Provide neither gold, nor silver, nor brass in your purses, nor scrip for your journey, neither two coats, neither shoes, nor yet staves: for the workman is worthy of his meat. And into whatsoever city or town ye shall enter, inquire who in it is worthy; and there abide till ye go thence. And when ye come into an house, salute it. And if the house be worthy, let your peace come upon it: but if it be not worthy, let your peace return to you. And whosoever shall not receive you, nor hear your words, when ye depart out of that house or city, shake off the dust of your feet. Verily I say unto you, It shall be more tolerable for the land of Sodom and Gomorrha in the day of judgment, than for that city.

Behold, I send you forth as sheep in the midst of wolves: be ye therefore wise as serpents, and harmless as doves. But beware of men: for they will deliver you up to the councils, and they will scourge you in their synagogues; and ye shall be brought before governors and kings for My sake, for a testimony against them and the Gentiles.

But when they deliver you up, take no thought how or what ye shall speak: for it shall be given you in that same hour what ye shall speak. For it is not ye that speak, but the Spirit of your Father which speaketh in you.

And the brother shall deliver up the brother to death, and the father the child: and the children shall rise up against their parents, and cause them to be put to death. And ye shall be hated of all men for My Name's sake: but he that endureth to the end shall be saved. But when they persecute you in this city, flee ye into another: for verily I say unto you, Ye shall not have gone over the cities of Israel, till the Son of man be come.

The disciple is not above his master, nor the servant above his lord. It is enough for the disciple that he be as his master, and the servant as his lord. If they have called the master of the house Beelzebub, how much more shall they call them of His household? Fear them not therefore: for there is nothing covered, that shall not be revealed; and hid, that shall not be known. What I tell you in darkness, that speak ye in light: and what ye hear in the ear, that preach ye upon the housetops. And fear not them which kill the body, but are not able to kill the soul: but rather fear Him which is able to destroy both soul and body in hell.

Are not two sparrows sold for a farthing? and one of them shall not fall on the ground without your Father. But the very hairs of your head are all numbered. Fear ye not therefore, ye are of more value than many sparrows.

Whosoever therefore shall confess Me before men, him will I confess also before My Father which is in heaven. But whosoever shall deny Me before men, him will I also deny before My Father which is in heaven.

Think not that I am come to send peace on earth: I came not to send peace, but a sword. For I am come to set a man at variance against his father, and the daughter against her mother, and the daughter in law against her mother in law. And a man's foes shall be they of his own household.

He that loveth father or mother more than Me is not worthy of Me: and he that loveth son or daughter more than Me is not worthy of Me. And he that taketh not his cross, and followeth after Me, is not worthy of Me. He that findeth his life shall lose it : and he that loseth his life for My sake shall find it.

He that receiveth you receiveth Me, and he that receiveth Me receiveth Him that sent Me. He that receiveth a prophet in the name of a prophet shall receive a prophet's reward; and he that receiveth a righteous man in the name of a righteous man shall receive a righteous man's reward. And whosoever shall give to drink unto one of these little ones a cup of cold water only in the name of a disciple, verily I say unto you, he shall in no wise lose his reward. *St. Matt.* x. 5–42.

(Cf. *St. Mark* vi. 8–11 ; *St. Luke* ix. 3–5.)

THIRD PERIOD.

FIRST PUBLIC MINISTRY IN GALILEE.

PART II.

From the return of the Twelve Apostles, March (?), A.D. 28, after their mission, to the close of the Galilæan ministry, October, A.D. 28.

JOURNEYINGS OF OUR LORD DURING THE THIRD PERIOD.

PART II.

From Capernaum to Desert Place near Bethsaida	St. Luke ix. 10.
Crosses the Lake to Capernaum	St. Matt. xiv. 34.
To Coasts of Tyre and Sidon	St. Matt. xv. 21.
Through Decapolis to Sea of Galilee	St. Mark vii. 31.
To the Parts of Dalmanutha	St. Mark viii. 10.
To Bethsaida	St. Mark viii. 22.
To Cæsarea Philippi	St. Mark viii. 27.
Mount Tabor	St. Mark ix. 2.
Through Galilee to Capernaum	St. Matt. xvii. 22, 24.

CHIEF EVENTS OF THIRD PERIOD.

PART II.

Return of the Twelve Apostles	St. Luke ix. 10.
Second Passover of our Lord's Public Life, March 28, A.D. 28, at which He was not present	St. John vi. 4.
Feeding the Five Thousand	St. Mark vi. 31–45.
Walking on the Water	St. Matt. xiv. 22–33.
The Great Discourse at Capernaum. Jesus abandoned by the Multitude and by many Disciples	St. John vi. 22–71.
The Woman of Canaan	St. Matt. xv. 22–28.
Healing of the Deaf Man	St. Mark vii. 31–37.
Second Miracle of the Loaves	St. Mark viii. 1–9.
Healing of Blind Man at Bethsaida	St. Mark viii. 22–26.
St. Peter's Great Confession	St. Matt. xvi. 13–20.
First Prediction of the Passion	St. Matt. xvi. 21–28.
The Transfiguration	St. Matt. xvii. 1–13.
Healing of the Maniac Boy	St. Mark ix. 14–27.
Second Prediction of the Passion	St. Mark ix. 30–32.
The Sacred Didrachma	St. Matt. xvii. 24–27.

Christ retires on hearing of St. John the Baptist's Death.

To the Twelve, on their Return.

Come ye yourselves apart into a desert place, and rest a while. *St. Mark* vi. 31.
(Cf. *St. Luke* ix. 10.)

First Miracle of the Loaves.
Desert near Bethsaida.

Disciples. *Send the multitude away.*

They need not depart; give ye them to eat.
St. Matt. xiv. 16.

To St. Philip.
Whence shall we buy bread, that these may eat?
St. John vi. 5.

Disciples. *Shall we go and buy?*

How many loaves have ye? go and see.
St. Mark vi. 38

Disciples. *Five, and two fishes.*

Bring them hither to Me. *St. Matt.* xiv. 18.
Make them sit down by fifties in a company.
St. Luke ix. 14.
(Cf. *St. John* vi. 10.)

When they were filled.

 Gather up the fragments that remain, that nothing be lost. *St. John* vi. 12.

Our Lord walks upon the Sea.

LAKE OF GENNESARET.

Disciples.   *It is a spirit.*

 Be of good cheer; it is I; be not afraid.
St. Matt. xiv. 27.

Peter.   *Lord, bid me come unto Thee.*

 Come.

Peter.   *Lord, save me.*

 O thou of little faith, wherefore didst thou doubt? *St. Matt.* xiv. 29, 31.

 (Cf. *St. Mark* vi. 50; *St. John* vi. 20.)

Discourse on the Day following.

CAPERNAUM.

The people.   *Rabbi, when camest Thou hither?*

 Verily, verily, I say unto you, Ye seek Me, not because ye saw the miracles, but because ye did eat of the loaves, and were filled. Labour not for the meat which perisheth, but for that meat which endureth unto everlasting life, which the Son of man shall give unto you: for Him hath God the Father sealed. *St. John* vi. 26, 27.

The people.   *What shall we do?*

 This is the work of God, that ye believe on Him whom He hath sent. *St. John* vi. 29

The people. *What sign showest Thou?*

Verily, verily, I say unto you, Moses gave you not that bread from heaven; but My Father giveth you the true bread from heaven. For the bread of God is He which cometh down from heaven, and giveth life unto the world.   *St. John* vi. 32, 33.

The people. *Lord, evermore give us this bread.*

I am the bread of life: he that cometh to Me shall never hunger; and he that believeth on Me shall never thirst. But I said unto you, That ye also have seen Me, and believe not. All that the Father giveth Me shall come to Me; and him that cometh to Me I will in no wise cast out.

For I came down from heaven, not to do Mine own will, but the will of Him that sent Me. And this is the Father's will which hath sent Me, that of all which He hath given Me I should lose nothing, but should raise it up again at the last day. And this is the will of Him that sent Me, that every one which seeth the Son, and believeth on Him, may have everlasting life: and I will raise him up at the last day.   *St. John* vi. 35-40.

The Jews. *Is not this the Son of Joseph?*

Murmur not among yourselves. No man can come to Me, except the Father which hath sent Me draw him: and I will raise him up at the last day. It is written in the prophets, And they shall be all taught of God. Every man therefore that hath heard, and hath learned of the Father, cometh unto Me. Not that any man hath seen the Father, save He which is of God, He hath seen the Father. Verily, verily, I say unto you, He that believeth on Me hath everlasting life.

I am that bread of life. Your fathers did eat

manna in the wilderness, and are dead. This is the bread which cometh down from heaven, that a man may eat thereof, and not die. I am the living bread which came down from heaven: if any man eat of this bread, he shall live for ever: and the bread that I will give is My flesh, which I will give for the life of the world. *St. John* vi. 43–51.

The Jews. How can this Man give us His flesh to eat?

Verily, verily, I say unto you, Except ye eat the flesh of the Son of man, and drink His blood, ye have no life in you. Whoso eateth My flesh, and drinketh My blood, hath eternal life; and I will raise him up at the last day. For My flesh is meat indeed, and My blood is drink indeed.

He that eateth My flesh, and drinketh My blood, dwelleth in Me, and I in him. As the living Father hath sent Me, and I live by the Father: so he that eateth Me, even he shall live by Me. This is that bread which came down from heaven: not as your fathers did eat manna, and are dead: he that eateth of this bread shall live for ever. *St. John* vi. 52–58.

Many disciples. This is an hard saying.

Doth this offend you? What and if ye shall see the Son of man ascend up where He was before? It is the Spirit that quickeneth; the flesh profiteth nothing: the words that I speak unto you, they are spirit, and they are life. But there are some of you that believe not. Therefore said I unto you, that no man can come unto Me, except it were given unto him of My Father.
St. John vi. 61–65.

To the Twelve.

Will ye also go away? *St. John* vi. 67.

Peter. Lord, to whom should we go?

Have not I chosen you twelve, and one of you is a devil? *St. John* vi. 70.

Warning to the Cities of Gennesaret.
CAPERNAUM.

Woe unto thee, Chorazin! woe unto thee, Bethsaida! for if the mighty works, which were done in you, had been done in Tyre and Sidon, they would have repented long ago in sackcloth and ashes. But I say unto you, It shall be more tolerable for Tyre and Sidon at the day of judgment, than for you.

And thou, Capernaum, which art exalted unto heaven, shalt be brought down to hell: for if the mighty works, which have been done in thee, had been done in Sodom, it would have remained until this day. But I say unto you, That it shall be more tolerable for the land of Sodom in the day of judgment, than for thee. *St. Matt.* xi. 21–24.

Thanksgiving.
CAPERNAUM.

I thank Thee, O Father, Lord of heaven and earth, because Thou hast hid these things from the wise and prudent, and hast revealed them unto babes. Even so, Father: for so it seemed good in Thy sight.

All things are delivered unto Me of My Father: and no man knoweth the Son, but the Father; neither knoweth any man the Father, save the Son, and he to whomsoever the Son will reveal Him. *St. Luke* x. 21, 22.

Invitation to the Heavy laden.

Come unto Me, all ye that are heavy laden, and I will give you rest. Take My yoke upon you, and learn of Me; for I am meek and lowly in heart: and ye shall find rest unto your souls. For My yoke is easy, and My burden is light.
St. Matt. xi. 28–30.

Eating with Unwashen Hands.

CAPERNAUM.

Pharisees and scribes from Jerusalem. Why do Thy disciples transgress the tradition?

Ye hypocrites, well did Esaias prophesy of you, saying, This people draweth nigh unto Me with their mouth, and honoureth Me with their lips; but their heart is far from Me. But in vain they do worship Me, teaching for doctrines the commandments of men. *St. Matt.* xv. 7–9.

For laying aside the commandment of God, ye hold the tradition of men, as the washing of pots and cups: and many other such like things ye do.
St. Mark vii. 8.

Why do ye also transgress the commandment of God,[1] that ye may keep your own tradition? For

Moses said, Honour thy father and thy mother; and, Whoso curseth father or mother, let him die the death: but ye say, If a man shall say to his father or mother, It is Corban, that is to say, a gift, by whatsoever thou mightest be profited by me;[2] and honour not his father or his mother, he shall be free.[3]

[1] *St. Matt.* xv. 3; [2] *St. Mark* vii. 9–11; [3] *St. Matt.* xv. 6.

And ye suffer him no more to do aught for his father or his mother; making the word of God of none effect through your tradition, which ye have delivered: and many such like things do ye.

St. Mark vii. 12, 13.

Discourse on Pollution.

CAPERNAUM.

To all the People.

Hearken unto Me every one of you, and understand: There is nothing from without a man, that entering into him can defile him: but the things which come out of him, those are they that defile the man. If any man have ears to hear, let him hear.

St. Mark vii. 14–16.
(Cf. *St. Matt.* xv. 10, 11.)

IN THE HOUSE WITH HIS DISCIPLES.

Disciples. Knowest Thou that the Pharisees were offended?

Every plant, which My heavenly Father hath not planted, shall be rooted up. Let them alone: they be blind leaders of the blind. And if the blind lead the blind, both shall fall into the ditch.

St. Matt. xv. 13, 14.

Peter. *Declare unto us this parable.*

Are ye so without understanding also? Do ye not perceive, that whatsoever thing from without entereth into the man, it cannot defile him; because it entereth not into his heart, but into the belly, and goeth out into the draught, purging all meats? For from within, out of the heart of men, proceed evil thoughts, adulteries, fornications, murders, thefts, covetousness, wickedness, deceit, lasciviousness, an evil eye, blasphemy, pride, foolishness: all these evil things come from within, and defile the man:[1] but to eat with unwashen hands defileth not a man.[2]

[1] *St. Mark* vii. 18-23; [2] *St. Matt.* xv. 20.

The Woman of Canaan.

PHŒNICIA.

April to July, A.D. 28.

Woman. *Have mercy on me.*

Disciples. *Send her away.*

I am not sent but unto the lost sheep of the house of Israel. *St. Matt.* xv. 24.

Woman. *Lord, help me.*

Let the children first be filled: for it is not meet to take the children's bread, and cast it unto the dogs. *St. Mark* vii. 27.

Woman. *Yet the dogs eat of the crumbs which fall from their masters' table.*

O woman, great is thy faith: be it unto thee even as thou wilt.[1] For this saying go thy way: the devil is gone out of thy daughter.[2]

[1] *St. Matt.* xv. 28; [2] *St. Mark* vii. 29.

Deaf and Stammering Man healed.
DECAPOLIS.

Ephphatha.   *St. Mark* vii. 34.

Second Miracle of the Loaves.
GENNESARET.

To the Disciples.

I have compassion on the multitude, because they continue with Me now three days, and have nothing to eat: and I will not send them away fasting, lest they faint in the way:[1] for divers of them came from far.[2]

             [1] *St. Matt.* xv. 32; [2] *St. Mark* viii. 3.

Disciples.   *Whence should we have so much bread?*

How many loaves have ye?   *St. Mark* viii. 5.

Disciples. Seven, and a few little fishes.

Pharisees and Sadducees again seek a Sign.
DALMANUTHA.

When it is evening, ye say, It will be fair weather: for the sky is red. And in the morning, It will be foul weather to-day: for the sky is red and lowring. O ye hypocrites, ye can discern the face of the sky; but can ye not discern the signs of the times? A wicked and adulterous generation seeketh after a sign; and there shall no sign be given unto it, but the sign of the prophet Jonas.   *St. Matt.* xvi. 2–4.
                             (Cf. *St. Mark* viii. 12.)

The Leaven of Scripture interpreted.

GENNESARET.

Take heed and beware of the leaven of the Pharisees and of the Sadducees,[1] and of the leaven of Herod.[2]   [1] *St. Matt.* xvi. 6; [2] *St. Mark* viii. 15.

Disciples.   *It is because we have taken no bread.*

O ye of little faith, why reason ye among yourselves, because ye have brought no bread?
St. Matt. xvi. 8.

Perceive ye not yet, neither understand? have ye your heart yet hardened? Having eyes, see ye not? and having ears, hear ye not? and do ye not remember? When I brake the five loaves among five thousand, how many baskets full of fragments took ye up?

Disciples.   *Twelve.*

And when the seven among four thousand, how many baskets full of fragments took ye up?
St. Mark viii. 17–20.

Disciples.   *Seven.*

How is it that ye do not understand that I spake it not to you concerning bread, that ye should beware of the leaven of the Pharisees and of the Sadducees?   *St. Matt.* xvi. 11.

Healing of the Blind at Bethsaida.

To the Man healed.

Neither go into the town, nor tell it to any in the town.   *St. Mark* viii. 26.

St. Peter's Great Confession.

Near Cæsarea Philippi.

Whom do men say that I the Son of man am?
Disciples. *John the Baptist; but some say Elias, etc.*
But whom say ye that I am?
Peter. *Thou art the Christ.*

Blessed art thou, Simon Bar-jona: for flesh and blood hath not revealed it unto thee, but My Father which is in heaven. And I say also unto thee, That thou art Peter, and upon this rock will I build My Church; and the gates of hell shall not prevail against it. And I will give unto thee the keys of the kingdom of heaven: and whatsoever thou shalt bind on earth shall be bound in heaven: and whatsoever thou shalt loose on earth shall be loosed in heaven.

St. Matt. xvi. 13, 15, 17-19.
(Cf. *St. Mark* viii. 27-29; *St. Luke* ix. 18-20.)

The Passion foretold.

To the Disciples.

The Son of man must suffer many things, and be rejected of the elders and chief priests and scribes, and be slain, and be raised the third day.

St. Luke ix. 22.

Peter. *Be it far from Thee, Lord.*

Get thee behind Me, Satan: thou art an offence unto Me: for thou savourest not the things that be of God, but those that be of men. *St. Matt.* xvi. 23.

To the People with the Disciples.

Whosoever will come after Me, let him deny himself, and take up his cross, and follow Me. For whosoever will save his life shall lose it; but whosoever shall lose his life for My sake and the gospel's, the same shall save it. For what shall it profit a man, if he shall gain the whole world, and lose his own soul? Or what shall a man give in exchange for his soul?

Whosoever therefore shall be ashamed of Me and of My words in this adulterous and sinful generation; of him also shall the Son of man be ashamed, when He cometh in the glory of His Father with the holy angels. *St. Mark* viii. 34–38.
(Cf. *St. Matt.* xvi. 24–26.)

And then He shall reward every man according to his works. Verily I say unto you, There be some standing here, which shall not taste of death, till they see the Son of man coming in His kingdom. *St. Matt.* xvi. 27, 28.

The Transfiguration.

To the Three Disciples.

Arise, and be not afraid.

Tell the vision to no man, until the Son of man be risen again from the dead.

Disciples. Why then say the scribes that Elias must first come?

Elias truly shall first come and restore all things. But I say unto you, That Elias is come already, and they knew him not, but have done unto him whatsoever they listed. Likewise shall also the Son of man suffer of them.

St. Matt. xvii. 7, 9, 11, 12.
(Cf. *St. Mark* ix. 12, 13.)

The Maniac Boy.

To the Scribes.

What question ye with them? *St. Mark* ix. 16.

One of the multitude. Lord, have mercy on my son.

O faithless and perverse generation, how long shall I be with you? how long shall I suffer you? bring him hither to Me. *St. Matt.* xvii. 17.

To the Father of the Boy.

How long is it ago since this came unto him?

The father. Of a child. If Thou canst do anything, help us.

If thou canst believe, all things are possible to him that believeth.

The father. Lord, I believe.

Thou dumb and deaf spirit, I charge thee, come out of him, and enter no more into him.

St. Mark ix. 21–25.

In the House privately.

Disciples. Why could not we cast him out?

Because of your unbelief: for verily I say unto you, If ye have faith as a grain of mustard seed, ye shall say unto this mountain, Remove hence to yonder place; and it shall remove; and nothing shall be impossible unto you. Howbeit this kind goeth not out but by prayer and fasting.

St. Matt. xvii. 20, 21.

The Passion again foretold.

ON THE WAY TO CAPERNAUM.

August, A.D. 28.

To the Disciples.

Let these sayings sink down into your ears: for the Son of man shall be delivered into the hands of men.[1] And they shall kill Him; and after that He is killed, He shall rise the third day.[2]

[1] *St. Luke* ix. 44; [2] *St. Mark* ix. 31.

The Sacred Didrachma.

CAPERNAUM.

To St. Peter.

What thinkest thou, Simon? of whom do the kings of the earth take custom or tribute? of their own children, or of strangers?

Peter.   Of strangers.

Then are the children free. Notwithstanding, lest we should offend them, go thou to the sea, and cast an hook, and take up the fish that first cometh up; and when thou hast opened his mouth, thou shalt find a piece of money: that take, and give unto them for Me and thee.

St. Matt. xvii. 25–27.

Which shall be the Greatest

CAPERNAUM.

To the Disciples in the House.

What was it that ye disputed among yourselves

by the way? If a man desire to be first, the same shall be last of all, and servant of all.

St. Mark ix. 33, 35.

Disciples. Who is the greatest in the kingdom of heaven?

Verily I say unto you, Except ye be converted, and become as little children, ye shall not enter into the kingdom of heaven. Whosoever therefore shall humble himself as this little child, the same is greatest in the kingdom of heaven. And whoso shall receive one such little child in My Name receiveth Me:[1] and whosoever shall receive Me, receiveth Him that sent Me: for he that is least among you all, the same shall be great.[2]

[1] *St. Matt.* xviii. 3–5; [2] *St. Luke* ix. 48.
(Cf. *St. Mark* ix. 37.)

"Forbid him not."

John. We saw one casting out devils in Thy Name, and we forbad him.

Forbid him not: for there is no man which shall do a miracle in My Name, that can lightly speak evil of Me. For he that is not against us is on our part. For whosoever shall give you a cup of water to drink in My Name, because ye belong to Christ, verily I say unto you, he shall not lose his reward. *St. Mark* ix. 39–41.

But whoso shall offend one of these little ones which believe in Me, it were better for him that a millstone were hanged about his neck, and that he were drowned in the depth of the sea.

Woe unto the world because of offences! for

it must needs be that offences come; but woe to that man by whom the offence cometh!

St. Matt. xviii. 6, 7.

And if thy hand offend thee, cut it off: it is better for thee to enter into life maimed, than having two hands to go into hell, into the fire that never shall be quenched: where their worm dieth not, and the fire is not quenched.

And if thy foot offend thee, cut it off: it is better for thee to enter halt into life, than having two feet to be cast into hell, into the fire that never shall be quenched: where their worm dieth not, and the fire is not quenched.

And if thine eye offend thee, pluck it out: it is better for thee to enter into the kingdom of God with one eye, than having two eyes to be cast into hell fire: where their worm dieth not, and the fire is not quenched.

For every one shall be salted with fire, and every sacrifice shall be salted with salt. Salt is good: but if the salt have lost his saltness, wherewith will ye season it? Have salt in yourselves, and have peace one with another. *St. Mark* ix. 43–50.

(Cf. *St. Matt.* xviii. 89.)

The Parable of Forgiveness.

Take heed that ye despise not one of these little ones; for I say unto you, That in heaven their angels do always behold the face of My Father which is in heaven. For the Son of man is come to save that which was lost.

How think ye? if a man have an hundred sheep, and one of them be gone astray, doth he not leave the ninety and nine, and goeth into the mountains, and seeketh that which is gone astray? And if so be that he find it, verily I say unto you, he rejoiceth more of that sheep, than of the ninety and nine which went not astray. Even so it is not the will of your Father which is in heaven, that one of these little ones should perish.

Moreover if thy brother shall trespass against thee, go and tell him his fault between thee and him alone: if he shall hear thee, thou hast gained thy brother. But if he will not hear thee, then take with thee one or two more, that in the mouth of two or three witnesses every word may be established. And if he shall neglect to hear them, tell it unto the Church: but if he neglect to hear the Church, let him be unto thee as an heathen man and a publican.

Verily I say unto you, Whatsoever ye shall bind on earth shall be bound in heaven: and whatsoever ye shall loose on earth shall be loosed in heaven.

Again I say unto you, That if two of you shall agree on earth as touching any thing that they shall ask, it shall be done for them of My Father which is in heaven. For where two or three are gathered together in My Name, there am I in the midst of them.

Peter. Lord, how oft shall my brother sin against me, and I forgive him? till seven times?

I say not unto thee, Until seven times: but, Until seventy times seven.

Therefore is the kingdom of heaven likened unto a certain king, which would take account of his servants. And when he had begun to reckon, one was brought unto him, which owed him ten thousand talents. But forasmuch as he had not to pay, his lord commanded him to be sold, and his wife, and children, and all that he had, and payment to be made. The servant therefore fell down, and worshipped him, saying, Lord, have patience with me, and I will pay thee all. Then the lord of that servant was moved with compassion, and loosed him, and forgave him the debt.

But the same servant went out, and found one of his fellow-servants, which owed him an hundred pence: and he laid hands on him, and took him by the throat, saying, Pay me that thou owest. And his fellow-servant fell down at his feet, and besought him, saying, Have patience with me, and I will pay thee all. And he would not: but went and cast him into prison, till he should pay the debt.

So when his fellow-servants saw what was done, they were very sorry, and came and told unto their lord all that was done. Then his lord, after that he had called him, said unto him, O thou wicked servant, I forgave thee all that debt, because thou desiredst me: shouldest not thou also have had compassion on thy fellow-servant, even as I had pity on thee?

And his lord was wroth, and delivered him to the tormentors, till he should pay all that was due unto him. So likewise shall My heavenly Father do also unto you, if ye from your hearts forgive not every one his brother their trespasses.

St. Matt. xviii. 10–35.

FOURTH PERIOD.

(JUDÆAN MINISTRY.)

From the final departure of Jesus from Galilee to go to the Feast of Tabernacles at Jerusalem (October 29, A.D. 28), to the last Passover, April, A.D. 29.

PART I.

From the departure from Galilee to the Feast of Dedication, December 20, A.D. 28.

JOURNEYINGS OF OUR LORD DURING THE FOURTH PERIOD.

PART I.

From Galilee through Samaria and Jericho to Jerusalem . . . . . . *St. John* vii. 2, 10; *St. Luke* ix. 51, 52.
To Peræa on East Side of Jordan.[1]
Return to Jerusalem for Feast of Dedication.
St. John x. 22.

CHIEF EVENTS DURING THE FOURTH PERIOD.

PART I.

Rejection by the Samaritans . . . . . *St. Luke* ix. 52-56.
Mission of the Seventy . . . . . *St. Luke* x. 1-16.
Jesus received by Martha . . . . . . *St. Luke* x. 38-42.
Discourses in the Temple during the Feast of Tabernacles . . . . *St. John* vii. 14-53.

---

[1] This retirement to Peræa, after the healing of the man born blind, is not mentioned directly in the Gospels; but it is thought to have taken place between the Feasts of Tabernacles and of Dedication, since in St. Luke xiii. 31 our Lord is warned to depart from Herod's territories. It is also said (St. Luke x. 1) that the Seventy were sent "into every city and place whither He Himself would come;" and Peræa, where He certainly went *after* the Feast of Dedication (St. John x. 40), had not yet been evangelized by Him. The conclusion of learned commentators is therefore here adopted, that our Lord retired to Peræa after the healing of the man born blind had stirred up the enmity of the Pharisees; was there joined by the Seventy, and that the events recorded in St. Luke x. 17–xiii. 33 took place at this time, *i.e.* from the end of October to middle of December, A.D. 28; Jesus returning to Jerusalem for the Feast of Dedication (December 20; St. John x. 22), and returning again to Peræa (St. John x. 40)—a journey which falls within the next period.

THE WOMAN TAKEN IN ADULTERY . . . . *St. John* viii. 2-11.
RENEWED DISCOURSES IN THE TEMPLE; JESUS DECLARES
    HIMSELF THE LIGHT OF THE WORLD . . *St. John* viii. 12-59.
THE MAN BLIND FROM HIS BIRTH HEALED . . . *St. John* ix.
RETURN OF THE SEVENTY (IN PERÆA?) . . *St. Luke* x. 17-24.
FRESH CONFLICTS WITH THE PHARISEES . . *St. Luke* xi. 14-26.
JESUS DINES WITH A PHARISEE . . . . . *St. Luke* xi. 37-54.
DISCOURSES TO DISCIPLES AND TO THE PEOPLE . . *St. Luke* xii.
THE WOMAN BOWED DOWN HEALED . . . *St. Luke* xiii. 11-17.

Before the Feast of Tabernacles.

GALILEE.

October, A.D. 28.

His brethren. Depart hence, and go into Judæa.

My time is not yet come: but your time is alway ready. The world cannot hate you; but Me it hateth, because I testify of it, that the works thereof are evil. Go ye up unto this feast: I go not up yet unto this feast; for My time is not yet full come. *St. John* vii. 6–8.

Rejected by the Samaritans.

IN A VILLAGE OF THE SAMARITANS.

James and John. Lord, wilt Thou that we command fire to come down from heaven?

Ye know not what manner of spirit ye are of. For the Son of man is not come to destroy men's lives, but to save them. *St. Luke* ix. 55, 56

The Seventy sent forth.

The harvest truly is great, but the labourers are few: pray ye therefore the Lord of the harvest, that He would send forth labourers into His harvest.

Go your ways: behold, I send you forth as lambs among wolves. Carry neither purse, nor scrip, nor shoes: and salute no man by the way. And into whatsoever house ye enter, first say, Peace be to this house. And if the son of peace be there, your peace shall rest upon it: if not, it shall turn to you again. And in the same house remain, eating and drinking such things as they give: for the labourer is worthy of his hire. Go not from house to house.

And into whatsoever city ye enter, and they receive you, eat such things as are set before you: and heal the sick that are therein, and say unto them, The kingdom of God is come nigh unto you. But into whatsoever city ye enter, and they receive you not, go your ways out into the streets of the same, and say, Even the very dust of your city, which cleaveth on us, we do wipe off against you: notwithstanding be ye sure of this, that the kingdom of God is come nigh unto you. But I say unto you, that it shall be more tolerable in that day for Sodom, than for that city.

Woe unto thee, Chorazin! woe unto thee, Bethsaida! for if the mighty works had been done in Tyre and Sidon, which have been done in you, they had a great while ago repented, sitting in sackcloth and ashes. But it shall be more tolerable for Tyre and Sidon at the judgment, than for you.

And thou, Capernaum, which art exalted to heaven, shalt be thrust down to hell. He that heareth you heareth Me; and he that despiseth you despiseth Me; and he that despiseth Me despiseth Him that sent Me. *St. Luke* x. 2–16.

Parable of the Good Samaritan.

On the Way to Jerusalem.
October, A.D. 28.

A certain lawyer. *What shall I do to inherit eternal life?*

What is written in the Law? how readest thou?

The lawyer. *Thou shalt love the Lord thy God, etc.*

Thou hast answered right: this do, and thou shalt live.

Lawyer. *And who is my neighbour?*

A certain man went down from Jerusalem to Jericho, and fell among thieves, which stripped him of his raiment, and wounded him, and departed, leaving him half dead.

And by chance there came down a certain priest that way: and when he saw him, he passed by on the other side. And likewise a Levite, when he was at the place, came and looked on him, and passed by on the other side.

But a certain Samaritan, as he journeyed, came where he was: and when he saw him, he had compassion on him, and went to him, and bound up his wounds, pouring in oil and wine, and set him on his own beast, and brought him to an inn, and took care of him. And on the morrow when he departed, he took out two pence, and gave them to the host, and said unto him, Take care of him; and whatsoever thou spendest more, when I come again, I will repay thee.

Which now of these three, thinkest thou, was neighbour unto him that fell among the thieves?

The lawyer. *He that showed mercy on him.*

Go, and do thou likewise. *St. Luke* x. 25-37.

The Disciples taught to pray.

Disciples. Lord, teach us to pray.

When ye pray, say, Our Father which art in heaven, Hallowed be Thy Name. Thy kingdom come. Thy will be done, as in heaven, so in earth. Give us day by day our daily bread. And forgive us our sins; for we also forgive every one that is indebted to us. And lead us not into temptation; but deliver us from evil.

Which of you shall have a friend, and shall go unto him at midnight, and say unto him, Friend, lend me three loaves; for a friend of mine in his journey is come to me, and I have nothing to set before him? And he from within shall answer and say, Trouble me not: the door is now shut, and my children are with me in bed; I cannot rise and give thee. I say unto you, Though he will not rise and give him, because he is his friend, yet because of his importunity he will rise and give him as many as he needeth.

And I say unto you, Ask, and it shall be given you; seek, and ye shall find; knock, and it shall be opened unto you. For every one that asketh receiveth; and he that seeketh findeth; and to him that knocketh it shall be opened.

If a son shall ask bread of any of you that is a father, will he give him a stone? or if he ask a fish, will he for a fish give him a serpent? or if he shall ask an egg, will he offer him a scorpion? If ye then, being evil, know how to give good gifts unto your children: how much more shall your heavenly Father give the Holy Spirit to them that ask Him? *St. Luke* xi. 1–13.

Martha and Mary.

Bethany.

Martha.   Lord, my sister hath left me to serve alone.

Martha, Martha, thou art careful and troubled about many things: but one thing is needful: and Mary hath chosen that good part, which shall not be taken away from her.   *St. Luke* x. 41, 42.

At the Feast of Tabernacles.

Jerusalem: in the Temple.

To the People.

My doctrine is not Mine, but His that sent Me. If any man will do His will, he shall know of the doctrine, whether it be of God, or whether I speak of Myself. He that speaketh of himself seeketh his own glory: but He that seeketh His glory that sent Him, the same is true, and no unrighteousness is in Him.

Did not Moses give you the Law, and yet none of you keepeth the Law? Why do ye go about to kill Me?

The people.   Who goeth about to kill Thee?

I have done one work, and ye all marvel. Moses therefore gave unto you circumcision; (not because it is of Moses, but of the fathers;) and ye on the sabbath day circumcise a man. If a man on the sabbath day receive circumcision, that the Law of Moses should not be broken; are ye angry at Me, because I have made a man every whit whole on the sabbath day? Judge not according to the appearance, but judge righteous judgment. *St. John* vii. 16–24.

"*Them of Jerusalem.*" *When Christ cometh, no man knoweth whence He is.*

Ye both know Me, and ye know whence I am: and I am not come of Myself, but He that sent Me is true, whom ye know not. But I know Him: for I am from Him, and He hath sent Me.
St. John vii. 28, 29.

(*Officers sent to take Him.*)

Yet a little while am I with you, and then I go unto Him that sent Me. Ye shall seek Me, and shall not find Me: and where I am, thither ye cannot come. *St. John* vii. 33, 34.

Last Day of the Feast.

If any man thirst, let him come unto Me, and drink. He that believeth on Me, as the Scripture hath said, out of his belly shall flow rivers of living water. *St. John* vii. 37, 38.

The Woman taken in Adultery.

The Temple.

To the Pharisees.

He that is without sin among you, let him first cast a stone at her.

To the Woman.

Woman, where are those thine accusers? hath no man condemned thee?

The woman.   *No man, Lord.*

    Neither do I condemn thee: go, and sin no more.   *St. John* viii. 7, 10, 11.

In the Treasury, as He taught in the Temple.

    I am the Light of the world: he that followeth Me shall not walk in darkness, but shall have the light of life.

Pharisees.   *Thou bearest record of Thyself; Thy record is not true.*

    Though I bear record of Myself, yet My record is true: for I know whence I came, and whither I go; but ye cannot tell whence I come, and whither I go. Ye judge after the flesh; I judge no man. And yet if I judge, My judgment is true: for I am not alone, but I and the Father that sent Me.

    It is also written in your Law, that the testimony of two men is true. I am One that bear witness of Myself, and the Father that sent Me beareth witness of Me.

Pharisees.   *Where is Thy Father?*

    Ye neither know Me, nor My Father: if ye had known Me, ye should have known My Father also.

    I go My way, and ye shall seek Me, and shall die in your sins: whither I go, ye cannot come.

The Jews.   *Will He kill Himself?*

    Ye are from beneath; I am from above: ye are of this world; I am not of this world. I said therefore unto you, that ye shall die in your sins: for if ye believe not that I am He, ye shall die in your sins.

The Jews. Who art Thou?

Even the same that I said unto you from the beginning. I have many things to say and to judge of you: but He that sent Me is true; and I speak to the world those things which I have heard of Him.

When ye have lifted up the Son of man, then shall ye know that I am He, and that I do nothing of Myself; but as My Father hath taught Me, I speak these things. And He that sent Me is with Me: the Father hath not left Me alone; for I do always those things that please Him.

St. John viii. 12, 14–19, 21, 23–26, 28, 29.

To the Jews which believed on Him.

If ye continue in My word, then are ye My disciples indeed; and ye shall know the truth, and the truth shall make you free. *St. John* viii. 31, 32.

The Jews. We were never in bondage to any man.

Verily, verily, I say unto you, Whosoever committeth sin is the servant of sin. And the servant abideth not in the house for ever: but the Son abideth ever. If the Son therefore shall make you free, ye shall be free indeed.

I know that ye are Abraham's seed; but ye seek to kill Me, because My word hath no place in you. I speak that which I have seen with My Father: and ye do that which ye have seen with your father. *St. John* viii. 34–38.

The Jews. Abraham is our father.

If ye were Abraham's children, ye would do the works of Abraham. But now ye seek to kill Me, a Man that hath told you the truth, which I have heard of God: this did not Abraham. Ye do the deeds of your father. *St. John* viii. 39-41.

The Jews. We have one Father, even God.

If God were your Father, ye would love Me: for I proceeded forth and came from God; neither came I of Myself, but He sent Me. Why do ye not understand My speech? even because ye cannot hear My word. Ye are of your father the devil, and the lusts of your father ye will do. He was a murderer from the beginning, and abode not in the truth, because there is no truth in him. When he speaketh a lie, he speaketh of his own: for he is a liar, and the father of it. And because I tell you the truth, ye believe Me not. Which of you convinceth Me of sin? And if I say the truth, why do ye not believe Me? He that is of God heareth God's words: ye therefore hear them not, because ye are not of God. *St. John* viii. 42-47.

The Jews. Say we not well that Thou ... hast a devil?

I have not a devil; but I honour My Father, and ye do dishonour Me. And I seek not Mine own glory: there is One that seeketh and judgeth.

Verily, verily, I say unto you, If a man keep My saying, he shall never see death.

St. John viii. 49-51.

The Jews. Whom makest Thou Thyself?

If I honour Myself, My honour is nothing: it is My Father that honoureth Me; of whom ye say, that He is your God: yet ye have not known Him; but I know Him: and if I should say, I know Him not, I shall be a liar like unto you: but I know Him, and keep His saying. Your father Abraham rejoiced to see My day: and he saw it, and was glad.

The Jews. Thou art not yet fifty years old, and hast Thou seen Abraham?

Verily, verily, I say unto you, Before Abraham was, I am. *St. John* viii. 54–58.

The Man Blind from His Birth.

Disciples. Who did sin, this man, or his parents, that he was born blind?

Neither hath this man sinned, nor his parents: but that the works of God should be made manifest in him. I must work the works of Him that sent Me, while it is day: the night cometh, when no man can work. As long as I am in the world, I am the Light of the world.

To the Blind Man.

Go, wash in the pool of Siloam.

To the same, after he was cast out of the Synagogue.

Dost thou believe on the Son of God?

The man. Who is He, Lord, that I might believe on Him?

Thou hast both seen Him, and it is He that talketh with thee.

The man. Lord, I believe.

For judgment I am come into this world, that they which see not might see; and that they which see might be made blind.

Pharisees. Are we blind also?

If ye were blind, ye should have no sin: but now ye say, We see; therefore your sin remaineth. *St. John* ix. 3–5, 7, 35–41.

The Good Shepherd.

JERUSALEM.

Verily, verily, I say unto you, He that entereth not by the door into the sheepfold, but climbeth up some other way, the same is a thief and a robber. But he that entereth in by the door is the shepherd of the sheep. To him the porter openeth; and the sheep hear his voice: and he calleth his own sheep by name, and leadeth them out. And when he putteth forth his own sheep, he goeth before them, and the sheep follow him: for they know his voice. And a stranger will they not follow, but will flee from him: for they know not the voice of strangers.

Verily, verily, I say unto you, I am the Door of the sheep. All that ever came before Me are thieves and robbers: but the sheep did not hear them.

I am the Door: by Me if any man enter in, he shall be saved, and shall go in and out, and find pasture. The thief cometh not, but for to steal, and to kill, and to destroy: I am come that they might have life, and that they might have it more abundantly.

I am the good Shepherd: the good Shepherd giveth His life for the sheep. But he that is an hireling, and not the shepherd, whose own the sheep are not, seeth the wolf coming, and leaveth the sheep, and fleeth: and the wolf catcheth them, and scattereth the sheep. The hireling fleeth, because he is an hireling, and careth not for the sheep.

I am the good Shepherd, and know My sheep, and am known of Mine. As the Father knoweth

Me, even so know I the Father: and I lay down My life for the sheep. And other sheep I have, which are not of this fold: them also I must bring, and they shall hear My voice; and there shall be one fold, and one Shepherd.

Therefore doth My Father love Me, because I lay down My life, that I might take it again. No man taketh it from Me, but I lay it down of Myself. I have power to lay it down, and I have power to take it again. This commandment have I received of My Father. *St. John* x. 1-5, 7-18.

Return of the Seventy.

PERÆA.

November (?), A.D. 28.

The seventy. Lord, even the devils are subject unto us through Thy Name.

I beheld Satan as lightning fall from heaven. Behold, I give unto you power to tread on serpents and scorpions, and over all the power of the enemy: and nothing shall by any means hurt you. Notwithstanding in this rejoice not, that the spirits are subject unto you; but rather rejoice, because your names are written in heaven.

I thank Thee, O Father, Lord of heaven and earth, that Thou hast hid these things from the wise and prudent, and hast revealed them unto babes: even so, Father; for so it seemed good in Thy sight.

All things are delivered to Me of My Father: and no man knoweth who the Son is, but the Father; and who the Father is, but the Son, and he to whom the Son will reveal Him. *St. Luke* x. 18-22.

To the Disciples privately.

Blessed are the eyes which see the things that ye see: for I tell you, that many prophets and kings have desired to see those things which ye see, and have not seen them; and to hear those things which ye hear, and have not heard them.

St. Luke x. 23, 24.

Our Lord dines with a Pharisee.
PEREA.

(*Pharisee marvelled that He had not first washed.*)

Now do ye Pharisees make clean the outside of the cup and the platter; but your inward part is full of ravening and wickedness. Ye fools, did not He that made that which is without make that which is within also? But rather give alms of such things as ye have; and, behold, all things are clean unto you.

But woe unto you, Pharisees! for ye tithe mint and rue and all manner of herbs, and pass over judgment and the love of God: these ought ye to have done, and not to leave the other undone.

Woe unto you, Pharisees! for ye love the uppermost seats in the synagogues, and greetings in the markets.

Woe unto you, scribes and Pharisees, hypocrites! for ye are as graves which appear not, and the men that walk over them are not aware of them.

St. Luke xi. 39-44.

A lawyer. Master, thus saying Thou reproachest us also.

Woe unto you also, ye lawyers! for ye lade men with burdens grievous to be borne, and ye yourselves touch not the burdens with one of your fingers.

Woe unto you! for ye build the sepulchres of the prophets, and your fathers killed them. Truly ye bear witness that ye allow the deeds of your fathers: for they indeed killed them, and ye build their sepulchres.

Therefore also said the Wisdom of God, I will send them prophets and apostles, and some of them they shall slay and persecute: that the blood of all the prophets, which was shed from the foundation of the world, may be required of this generation; from the blood of Abel unto the blood of Zacharias, which perished between the altar and the temple: verily I say unto you, It shall be required of this generation.

Woe unto you, lawyers! for ye have taken away the key of knowledge: ye entered not in yourselves, and them that were entering in ye hindered.

St. Luke xi. 46–52.

Warning against Hypocrisy.

PERÆA.

To the Disciples.

Beware ye of the leaven of the Pharisees, which is hypocrisy. For there is nothing covered, that shall not be revealed; neither hid, that shall not be known. Therefore whatsoever ye have spoken in darkness shall be heard in the light; and that which ye have spoken in the ear in closets shall be proclaimed upon the housetops.

And I say unto you My friends, Be not afraid

of them that kill the body, and after that have no more that they can do. But I will forewarn you whom ye shall fear: Fear Him, which after He hath killed hath power to cast into hell; yea, I say unto you, Fear Him. Are not five sparrows sold for two farthings, and not one of them is forgotten before God? But even the very hairs of your head are all numbered. Fear not therefore: ye are of more value than many sparrows.

Also I say unto you, Whosoever shall confess Me before men, him shall the Son of man also confess before the angels of God: but he that denieth Me before men shall be denied before the angels of God.

And whosoever shall speak a word against the Son of man, it shall be forgiven him: but unto him that blasphemeth against the Holy Ghost it shall not be forgiven.

And when they bring you unto the synagogues, and unto magistrates, and powers, take ye no thought how or what thing ye shall answer, or what ye shall say: for the Holy Ghost shall teach you in the same hour what ye ought to say.

St. Luke xii. 1-12.

The Rich Fool.

PERÆA.

One of the company. Master, speak to my brother, that he divide the inheritance with me.

Man, who made Me a judge or a divider over you? *St. Luke* xii. 14.

To the Multitude.

Take heed, and beware of covetousness: for a man's life consisteth not in the abundance of the things which he possesseth.

The ground of a certain rich man brought forth plentifully: and he thought within himself, saying, What shall I do, because I have no room where to bestow my fruits? And he said, This will I do: I will pull down my barns, and build greater; and there will I bestow all my fruits and my goods. And I will say to my soul, Soul, thou hast much goods laid up for many years; take thine ease, eat, drink, and be merry.

But God said unto him, Thou fool, this night thy soul shall be required of thee: then whose shall those things be, which thou hast provided? So is he that layeth up treasure for himself, and is not rich toward God. *St. Luke* xii. 15-21.

To the Disciples.

Therefore I say unto you, Take no thought for your life, what ye shall eat; neither for the body, what ye shall put on. The life is more than meat, and the body is more than raiment. Consider the ravens: for they neither sow nor reap; which neither have storehouse nor barn; and God feedeth them: how much more are ye better than the fowls?

And which of you with taking thought can add to his stature one cubit? If ye then be not able to do that thing which is least, why take ye thought for the rest?

Consider the lilies how they grow: they toil not, they spin not; and yet I say unto you, that Solomon in all his glory was not arrayed like one of these. If then God so clothe the grass, which is to-day in the field, and to-morrow is cast into the oven; how much more will He clothe you, O ye of little faith?

And seek not ye what ye shall eat, or what ye shall drink, neither be ye of doubtful mind. For all these things do the nations of the world seek after: and your Father knoweth that ye have need of these things. But rather seek ye the kingdom of God; and all these things shall be added unto you. Fear not, little flock; for it is your Father's good pleasure to give you the kingdom.

Sell that ye have, and give alms; provide yourselves bags which wax not old, a treasure in the heavens that faileth not, where no thief approacheth, neither moth corrupteth. For where your treasure is, there will your heart be also.

Let your loins be girded about, and your lights burning; and ye yourselves like unto men that wait for their lord, when he will return from the wedding; that when he cometh and knocketh, they may open unto him immediately. Blessed are those servants, whom the lord when he cometh shall find watching: verily I say unto you, that he shall gird himself, and make them to sit down to meat, and will come forth and serve them. And if he shall come in the second watch, or come in the third watch, and find them so, blessed are those servants.

And this know, that if the goodman of the house had known what hour the thief would come, he would have watched, and not have suffered his house to be broken through. Be ye therefore ready also: for the Son of man cometh at an hour when ye think not.

Peter. Lord, speakest Thou this parable unto us, or even to all?

Who then is that faithful and wise steward, whom his lord shall make ruler over his household, to give them their portion of meat in due season? Blessed is that servant, whom his lord when he cometh shall find so doing. Of a truth I say unto you, that he will make him ruler over all that he hath.

But and if that servant say in his heart, My lord delayeth his coming; and shall begin to beat the menservants and maidens, and to eat and drink, and to be drunken; the lord of that servant will come in a day when he looketh not for him, and at an hour when he is not aware, and will cut him in sunder, and will appoint him his portion with the unbelievers.

And that servant, which knew his lord's will, and prepared not himself, neither did according to his will, shall be beaten with many stripes. But he that knew not, and did commit things worthy of stripes, shall be beaten with few stripes. For unto whomsoever much is given, of him shall be much required: and to whom men have committed much, of him they will ask the more.

I am come to send fire on the earth; and what will I, if it be already kindled? But I have a baptism to be baptized with; and how am I straitened till it be accomplished!

Suppose ye that I am come to give peace on earth? I tell you, Nay; but rather division: for from henceforth there shall be five in one house divided, three against two, and two against three. The father shall be divided against the son, and the son against the father; the mother against the daughter, and the daughter against the mother; the mother-in-law against her daughter-in-law, and the daughter-in-law against her mother-in-law.

To the People.

When ye see a cloud rise out of the west, straightway ye say, There cometh a shower; and so it is. And when ye see the south wind blow, ye say, There will be heat; and it cometh to pass. Ye hypocrites, ye can discern the face of the sky and of the earth; but how is it that ye do not discern this time? Yea, and why even of yourselves judge ye not what is right?

When thou goest with thine adversary to the magistrate, as thou art in the way, give diligence that thou mayest be delivered from him; lest he hale thee to the judge, and the judge deliver thee to the officer, and the officer cast thee into prison. I tell thee, thou shalt not depart thence, till thou hast paid the very last mite. *St. Luke* xii. 22-59.

The Galilæans slain by Pilate.

PERÆA.

Suppose ye that these Galilæans were sinners above all the Galilæans, because they suffered such things? I tell you, Nay: but, except ye repent, ye shall all likewise perish.

Or those eighteen, upon whom the tower in Siloam fell, and slew them, think ye that they were sinners above all men that dwelt in Jerusalem? I tell you, Nay: but, except ye repent, ye shall all likewise perish. *St. Luke* xiii. 2-5.

Parable of the Barren Fig Tree.

A certain man had a fig tree planted in his vineyard; and he came and sought fruit thereon, and found none. Then said he unto the dresser of his vineyard, Behold, these three years I come seeking fruit on this fig tree, and find none: cut it down; why cumbereth it the ground? And he answering said unto him, Lord, let it alone this year also, till I shall dig about it, and dung it: and if it bear fruit, well: and if not, then after that thou shalt cut it down. *St. Luke* xiii, 6–9.

The Woman bowed down with Infirmity.

Woman, thou art loosed from thine infirmity.

Ruler of synagogue. There are six days ... in them come and be healed, and not on the sabbath day.

Thou hypocrite, doth not each one of you on the sabbath loose his ox or his ass from the stall, and lead him away to watering? And ought not this woman, being a daughter of Abraham, whom Satan hath bound, lo, these eighteen years, be loosed from this bond on the sabbath day?
St. Luke xiii. 12, 15, 16.

FOURTH PERIOD.
PART II.

From the Feast of Dedication at Jerusalem, A.D. 28, to the arrival at Bethany, before the last Passover, end of March, A.D. 29.

JOURNEYINGS OF OUR LORD DURING THE FOURTH PERIOD.

PART II.

From Jerusalem to Bethabara beyond Jordan (in Peræa) . . . . *St. John* x. 40 (cf. ch. i. 28).
Return into Judæa to Bethany . . . *St. John* xi. 7, 17, 18.
To Ephraim . . . . *St. John* xi. 54.
By a Circuit through Samaria and Valley of Jordan towards Jerusalem . . . . *St. Luke* xiii. 22; xvii. 11.
To Jericho . . . . *St. Luke* xviii. 35.
From Jericho to Bethany . . . . *St. Mark* x. 46; xi. 1.

CHIEF EVENTS IN FOURTH PERIOD.

PART II.

Discourse in Solomon's Porch; Jesus asserts His Oneness with the Father . . . . . . *St. John* x. 22–39.
Sojourn in Peræa . . . . *St. John* x. 40–42.
Dines with a Pharisee, and heals a Man of the Dropsy. Discourses . . . . *St. Luke* xiv.
Parables and Teaching . *St. Luke* xv., xvi., xvii. 1–10.
Raising of Lazarus . . . . *St. John* xi. 1–46.
Retirement . . . . *St. John* xi. 54–57.
The Healing of Ten Lepers on the Last Journey to Jerusalem . . . . *St. Luke* xvii. 11–19.
Teaching and Parables . . *St. Luke* xvii. 20–37; xviii. 9–14.
The Blessing of the Little Children . *St. Luke* xviii. 15–17.
Third Prediction of the Passion . . *St. Luke* xviii. 31–34.
Request of the Sons of Zebedee . . . *St. Matt.* xx. 20–28.
Healing of Blind Man at Entry of Jericho
 St. Luke xviii. 35–43.
In the House of Zacchæus . . . . . *St. Luke* xix. 1–10.
Healing of Two Blind Men on leaving Jericho
 St. Matt. xx. 30–34.

The Feast of Dedication.

In Solomon's Porch in the Temple.

The Jews. If Thou be the Christ, tell us plainly.

I told you, and ye believed not: the works that I do in My Father's Name, they bear witness of Me. But ye believe not, because ye are not of My sheep, as I said unto you. My sheep hear My voice, and I know them, and they follow Me: and I give unto them eternal life; and they shall never perish, neither shall any man pluck them out of My hand. My Father, which gave them Me, is greater than all; and no man is able to pluck them out of My Father's hand. I and My Father are One.

(*They take up stones, to stone Him.*)

Many good works have I showed you from My Father; for which of those works do ye stone Me?

The Jews. Because that Thou, being a man, makest Thyself God.

Is it not written in your Law, I said, Ye are gods? If He called them gods, unto whom the word of God came, and the Scripture cannot be broken; say ye of Him, whom the Father hath sanctified, and sent into the world, Thou blasphemest; because I said, I am the Son of God?

If I do not the works of My Father, believe Me

not. But if I do, though ye believe not Me, believe the works: that ye may know, and believe, that the Father is in Me, and I in Him.

St. John x. 25-30, 32-38.

Dropsy healed on the Sabbath.
In the House of the Chief Pharisee: Peræa.
January, A.D. 29.

To the Lawyers and Pharisees.

Is it lawful to heal on the sabbath day?

(*They hold their peace.*)

Which of you shall have an ass or an ox fallen into a pit, and will not straightway pull him out on the sabbath day? *St. Luke* xiv. 3, 5.

Parables at the Feast.
To those choosing out the Chief Rooms.

When thou art bidden of any man to a wedding, sit not down in the highest room; lest a more honourable man than thou be bidden of him; and he that bade thee and him come and say to thee, Give this man place; and thou begin with shame to take the lowest room.

But when thou art bidden, go and sit down in the lowest room; that when he that bade thee cometh, he may say unto thee, Friend, go up higher: then shalt thou have worship in the presence of them that sit at meat with thee. For whosoever exalteth himself shall be abased; and he that humbleth himself shall be exalted.

St. Luke xiv. 8-11.

To His Host.

When thou makest a dinner or a supper, call not thy friends, nor thy brethren, neither thy kinsmen, nor thy rich neighbours; lest they also bid thee again, and a recompense be made thee.

But when thou makest a feast, call the poor, the maimed, the lame, the blind: and thou shalt be blessed; for they cannot recompense thee: for thou shalt be recompensed at the resurrection of the just. *St. Luke* xiv. 12–14.

Parable of the Great Supper.

One of those at table. Blessed is he that shall eat bread in the kingdom of God.

A certain man made a great supper, and bade many: and sent his servant at supper time to say to them that were bidden, Come; for all things are now ready.

And they all with one consent began to make excuse. The first said unto him, I have bought a piece of ground, and I must needs go and see it: I pray thee have me excused. And another said, I have bought five yoke of oxen, and I go to prove them: I pray thee have me excused. And another said, I have married a wife, and therefore I cannot come.

So that servant came, and showed his lord these things. Then the master of the house being angry said to his servant, Go out quickly into the streets and lanes of the city, and bring in hither the poor, and the maimed, and the halt, and the blind. And the servant said, Lord, it is done as thou hast commanded, and yet there is room.

And the lord said unto the servant, Go out into the highways and hedges, and compel them to come in, that my house may be filled. For I say unto you, That none of those men which were bidden shall taste of my supper. *St. Luke* xiv. 16–24.

To the Multitude following Him.

If any man come to Me, and hate not his father, and mother, and wife, and children, and brethren, and sisters, yea, and his own life also, he cannot be My disciple. And whosoever doth not bear his cross, and come after Me, cannot be My disciple.

For which of you, intending to build a tower, sitteth not down first, and counteth the cost, whether he have sufficient to finish it? Lest haply, after he hath laid the foundation, and is not able to finish it, all that behold it begin to mock him, saying, This man began to build, and was not able to finish.

Or what king, going to make war against another king, sitteth not down first, and consulteth whether he be able with ten thousand to meet him that cometh against him with twenty thousand? Or else, while the other is yet a great way off, he sendeth an ambassage, and desireth conditions of peace. So likewise, whosoever he be of you that forsaketh not all that he hath, he cannot be My disciple.

Salt is good: but if the salt have lost his savour, wherewith shall it be seasoned? It is neither fit for the land, nor yet for the dunghill; but men cast it out. He that hath ears to hear, let him hear. *St. Luke* xiv. 26–35.

The Lost Sheep.

Pharisees. This Man receiveth sinners.

What man of you, having an hundred sheep, if he lose one of them, doth not leave the ninety and nine in the wilderness, and go after that which is lost, until he find it? And when he hath found it, he layeth it on his shoulders, rejoicing. And when he cometh home, he calleth together his friends and neighbours, saying unto them, Rejoice with me; for I have found my sheep which was lost.

I say unto you, that likewise joy shall be in heaven over one sinner that repenteth, more than over ninety and nine just persons, which need no repentance.

Either what woman having ten pieces of silver, if she lose one piece, doth not light a candle, and sweep the house, and seek diligently till she find it? And when she hath found it, she calleth her friends and her neighbours together, saying, Rejoice with me; for I have found the piece which I had lost.

Likewise, I say unto you, there is joy in the presence of the angels of God over one sinner that repenteth. *St. Luke* xv. 4-10.

The Prodigal Son.

A certain man had two sons: and the younger of them said to his father, Father, give me the portion of goods that falleth to me. And he divided unto them his living.

And not many days after the younger son

gathered all together, and took his journey into a far country, and there wasted his substance with riotous living. And when he had spent all, there arose a mighty famine in that land; and he began to be in want. And he went and joined himself to a citizen of that country; and he sent him into his fields to feed swine. And he would fain have filled his belly with the husks that the swine did eat: and no man gave unto him. And when he came to himself, he said, How many hired servants of my father's have bread enough and to spare, and I perish with hunger! I will arise and go to my father, and will say unto him, Father, I have sinned against Heaven, and before thee, and am no more worthy to be called thy son: make me as one of thy hired servants.

And he arose, and came to his father. But when he was yet a great way off, his father saw him, and had compassion, and ran, and fell on his neck, and kissed him. And the son said unto him, Father, I have sinned against Heaven, and in thy sight, and am no more worthy to be called thy son.

But the father said to his servants, Bring forth the best robe, and put it on him; and put a ring on his hand, and shoes on his feet: and bring hither the fatted calf, and kill it; and let us eat, and be merry: for this my son was dead, and is alive again; he was lost, and is found. And they began to be merry.

Now his elder son was in the field: and as he came and drew nigh to the house, he heard musick and dancing. And he called one of the servants, and asked what these things meant. And he said unto him, Thy brother is come; and thy father hath killed the fatted calf, because he hath received him safe and sound. And he was angry, and would not go in: therefore came his father out, and intreated him.

And he answering said to his father, Lo, these many years do I serve thee, neither transgressed I at any time thy commandment: and yet thou never gavest me a kid, that I might make merry with my friends: but as soon as this thy son was come, which hath devoured thy living with harlots, thou hast killed for him the fatted calf.

And he said unto him, Son, thou art ever with me, and all that I have is thine. It was meet that we should make merry, and be glad: for this thy brother was dead, and is alive again; and was lost, and is found. *St. Luke* xv. 11–32.

The Unjust Steward.

To the Disciples.

There was a certain rich man, which had a steward; and the same was accused unto him that he had wasted his goods. And he called him, and said unto him, How is it that I hear this of thee? give an account of thy stewardship; for thou mayest be no longer steward.

Then the steward said within himself, What shall I do? for my lord taketh away from me the stewardship: I cannot dig; to beg I am ashamed. I am resolved what to do, that, when I am put out of the stewardship, they may receive me into their houses.

So he called every one of his lord's debtors unto him, and said unto the first, How much owest thou unto my lord? And he said, An hundred measures of oil. And he said unto him, Take thy bill, and sit down quickly, and write fifty. Then said he to another, And how much owest thou? And he said, An hundred measures of wheat. And he said unto him, Take thy bill, and write fourscore.

And the lord commended the unjust steward, because he had done wisely: for the children of this world are in their generation wiser than the children of light. And I say unto you, Make to yourselves friends of the mammon of unrighteousness; that, when ye fail, they may receive you into everlasting habitations.

He that is faithful in that which is least is faithful also in much: and he that is unjust in the least is unjust also in much. If therefore ye have not been faithful in the unrighteous mammon, who will commit to your trust the true riches? And if ye have not been faithful in that which is another man's, who shall give you that which is your own?

No servant can serve two masters: for either he will hate the one, and love the other; or else he will hold to the one, and despise the other. Ye cannot serve God and mammon.

St. Luke xvi. 1–13

On Divorce.

IN THE COASTS OF JUDÆA, BEYOND JORDAN.

Pharisees. Is it lawful for a man to put away his wife?
What did Moses command you?

Pharisees. To write a bill of divorcement, and to put her away.

For the hardness of your heart he wrote you this precept. But from the beginning of the creation God made them male and female. For this cause shall a man leave his father and mother, and cleave to his wife; and they twain shall be one flesh: so then they are no more twain, but one flesh. What therefore God hath joined together, let not man put asunder. *St. Mark* x. 3–9. (Cf. *St. Matt.* xix. 3–6.)

Pharisees. *Why did Moses then command to put her away?*

Moses because of the hardness of your hearts suffered you to put away your wives: but from the beginning it was not so. *St. Matt.* xix. 8.

To the Disciples in the House privately.

(*They ask Him again of the same matter.*)

I say unto you, Whosoever shall put away his wife, except it be for fornication, and shall marry another, committeth adultery: and whoso marrieth her which is put away doth commit adultery.[1] And if a woman shall put away her husband, and be married to another, she committeth adultery.[2]

[1] *St. Matt.* xix. 9; [2] *St. Mark* x. 12.

Disciples. *If the case be so . . . it is not good to marry.*

All men cannot receive this saying, save they to whom it is given. For there are some eunuchs, which were so born from their mother's womb: and there are some eunuchs, which were made eunuchs of men: and there be eunuchs which have made themselves eunuchs for the kingdom of heaven's sake. He that is able to receive it, let him receive it. *St. Matt.* xix. 11, 12.

Dives and Lazarus.

To the Covetous Pharisees.

Ye are they which justify yourselves before men; but God knoweth your hearts: for that which is highly esteemed among men is abomination in the sight of God.

The Law and the prophets were until John: since that time the kingdom of God is preached, and every man presseth into it. And it is easier for heaven and earth to pass, than one tittle of the law to fail.

Whosoever putteth away his wife, and marrieth another, committeth adultery: and whosoever marrieth her that is put away from her husband committeth adultery.

There was a certain rich man, which was clothed in purple and fine linen, and fared sumptuously every day: and there was a certain beggar named Lazarus, which was laid at his gate, full of sores, and desiring to be fed with the crumbs which fell from the rich man's table: moreover the dogs came and licked his sores.

And it came to pass, that the beggar died, and was carried by the angels into Abraham's bosom: the rich man also died, and was buried; and in hell he lift up his eyes, being in torments, and seeth Abraham afar off, and Lazarus in his bosom. And he cried and said, Father Abraham, have mercy on me, and send Lazarus, that he may dip the tip of his finger in water, and cool my tongue; for I am tormented in this flame.

But Abraham said, Son, remember that thou in thy lifetime receivedst thy good things, and likewise Lazarus evil things: but now he is comforted, and thou art tormented. And beside all this, between us and you there is a great gulf fixed: so that they which would pass from hence to you cannot; neither can they pass to us, that would come from thence.

Then he said, I pray thee therefore, father, that thou wouldest send him to my father's house: for I have five brethren; that he may testify unto them, lest they also come into this place of torment.

Abraham saith unto him, They have Moses and the prophets; let them hear them. And he said, Nay, father Abraham: but if one went unto them from the dead, they will repent. And he said unto him, If they hear not Moses and the prophets, neither will they be persuaded, though one rose from the dead. *St. Luke* xvi. 15-31.

Concerning Offences.

To the Disciples.

It is impossible but that offences will come: but woe unto him, through whom they come! It were better for him that a millstone were hanged about his neck, and he cast into the sea, than that he should offend one of these little ones.

Take heed to yourselves: If thy brother trespass against thee, rebuke him; and if he repent, forgive him. And if he trespass against thee seven times in a day, and seven times in a day turn again to thee, saying, I repent; thou shalt forgive him.

Apostles. Increase our faith.

If ye had faith as a grain of mustard seed, ye might say unto this sycamine tree, Be thou plucked up by the root, and be thou planted in the sea; and it should obey you.

But which of you, having a servant plowing or feeding cattle, will say unto him by and by, when he is come from the field, Go and sit down to meat? And will not rather say unto him, Make ready wherewith I may sup, and gird thyself, and serve me, till I have eaten and drunken; and afterward thou shalt eat and drink? Doth he thank that servant because he did the things that were commanded him? I trow not. So likewise ye, when ye shall have done all those things which are commanded you, say, We are unprofitable servants: we have done that which was our duty to do. *St. Luke* xvii. 1–10.

The Sickness of Lazarus.

February (?), A.D. 29.

To the Disciples.

This sickness is not unto death, but for the glory of God, that the Son of God might be glorified thereby.

To the same, after Two Days.

Let us go into Judæa again.

Disciples. *The Jews of late sought to stone Thee.*

Are there not twelve hours in the day? If any man walk in the day, he stumbleth not, because he seeth the light of this world. But if a man walk in the night, he stumbleth, because there is no light in him.

Our friend Lazarus sleepeth; but I go, that I may awake him out of sleep.

Disciples. *Lord, if he sleep, he shall do well.*

Lazarus is dead. And I am glad for your sakes that I was not there, to the intent ye may believe; nevertheless let us go unto him. *St. John* xi. 4-15.

Raising of Lazarus.

BETHANY.

To Martha.

Thy brother shall rise again.

Martha. *I know that he shall rise again in the resurrection.*

I am the Resurrection, and the Life: he that believeth in Me, though he were dead, yet shall he live: and whosoever liveth and believeth in Me shall never die. Believest thou this?

To Mary and the Mourners.

Where have ye laid him?

AT THE GRAVE.

Take ye away the stone.

Martha. *Lord, . . . he hath been dead four days.*

Said I not unto thee, that, if thou wouldest believe, thou shouldest see the glory of God?

Father, I thank Thee that Thou hast heard Me.

And I knew that Thou hearest Me always: but because of the people which stand by I said it, that they may believe that Thou hast sent Me.

(*With a loud voice.*)

Lazarus, come forth.

To the Mourners.

Loose him, and let him go.

St. *John* xi. 23–26, 34, 39–44.

On the Journey to Jerusalem.

One. Lord, are there few that be saved?

Strive to enter in at the strait gate: for many, I say unto you, will seek to enter in, and shall not be able. When once the master of the house is risen up, and hath shut to the door, and ye begin to stand without, and to knock at the door, saying, Lord, Lord, open unto us; and He shall answer and say unto you, I know you not whence ye are: then shall ye begin to say, We have eaten and drunk in Thy presence, and Thou hast taught in our streets.

But He shall say, I tell you, I know you not whence ye are; depart from Me, all ye workers of iniquity. There shall be weeping and gnashing of teeth, when ye shall see Abraham, and Isaac, and Jacob, and all the prophets, in the kingdom of God, and you yourselves thrust out.

And they shall come from the east, and from the west, and from the north, and from the south, and shall sit down in the kingdom of God. And, behold, there are last which shall be first, and there are first which shall be last.

The Pharisees. Depart hence, for Herod will kill Thee.

Go ye, and tell that fox, Behold, I cast out devils, and I do cures to-day and to-morrow, and the third day I shall be perfected. Nevertheless I must walk to-day, and to-morrow, and the day following: for it cannot be that a prophet perish out of Jerusalem.

O Jerusalem, Jerusalem, which killest the prophets, and stonest them that are sent unto thee; how often would I have gathered thy children together, as a hen doth gather her brood under her wings, and ye would not! Behold, your house is left unto you desolate: and verily I say unto you, Ye shall not see Me, until the time come when ye shall say, Blessed is He that cometh in the Name of the Lord. *St. Luke* xiii. 24–35.

The Ten Lepers.

ON THE JOURNEY THROUGH SAMARIA AND GALILEE.

To the Lepers.

Go show yourselves unto the priests.

(The Samaritan leper gives thanks.)

Were there not ten cleansed? but where are the nine?

There are not found that returned to give glory to God, save this stranger.

To the Samaritan.

Arise, go thy way: thy faith hath made thee whole. *St. Luke* xvii. 14, 17–20.

The Coming of the Kingdom.

To the Pharisees demanding when the Kingdom of God should come.

The kingdom of God cometh not with observation: neither shall they say, Lo here! or, lo there! for, behold, the kingdom of God is within you.

To the Disciples.

The days will come, when ye shall desire to see one of the days of the Son of man, and ye shall not see it. And they shall say unto you, See here; or, see there: go not after them, nor follow them. For as the lightning, that lighteneth out of the one part under heaven, shineth unto the other part under heaven; so shall also the Son of man be in His day. But first must He suffer many things, and be rejected of this generation.

And as it was in the days of Noe, so shall it be also in the days of the Son of man. They did eat, they drank, they married wives, they were given in marriage, until the day that Noe entered into the ark, and the flood came, and destroyed them all. Likewise also as it was in the days of Lot; they did eat, they drank, they bought, they sold, they planted, they builded; but the same day that Lot went out of Sodom it rained fire and brimstone from heaven, and destroyed them all. Even thus shall it be in the day when the Son of man is revealed.

In that day, he which shall be upon the housetop, and his stuff in the house, let him not come down to take it away; and he that is in the field, let him likewise not return back.

Remember Lot's wife. Whosoever shall seek to save his life shall lose it; and whosoever shall lose his life shall preserve it.

I tell you, in that night there shall be two men in one bed; the one shall be taken, and the other shall be left. Two women shall be grinding together; the one shall be taken, and the other left. Two men shall be in the field; the one shall be taken, and the other left.

Disciples. *Where, Lord?*

Wheresoever the body is, thither will the eagles be gathered together. *St. Luke* xvii. 20–37.

The Importunate Widow.

To the Disciples.

There was in a city a judge, which feared not God, neither regarded man: and there was a widow in that city; and she came unto him, saying, Avenge me of mine adversary. And he would not for a while: but afterward he said within himself, Though I fear not God, nor regard man; yet because this widow troubleth me, I will avenge her, lest by her continual coming she weary me.

Hear what the unjust judge saith. And shall not God avenge His own elect, which cry day and night unto Him, though He bear long with them? I tell you that He will avenge them speedily. Nevertheless when the Son of man cometh, shall He find faith on the earth? *St. Luke* xviii. 2–8.

The Pharisee and the Publican.

To Certain Self-righteous, who despised others.

Two men went up into the temple to pray; the one a Pharisee, and the other a publican. The Pharisee stood and prayed thus with himself, God, I thank Thee, that I am not as other men are, extortioners, unjust, adulterers, or even as this publican. I fast twice in the week, I give tithes of all that I possess.

And the publican, standing afar off, would not lift up so much as his eyes unto heaven, but smote upon his breast, saying, God be merciful to me a sinner. I tell you, this man went down to his house justified rather than the other: for every one that exalteth himself shall be abased; and he that humbleth himself shall be exalted.

St. Luke xviii. 10–14.

Infants brought to Christ.

To the Disciples.

Suffer the little children to come unto Me, and forbid them not: for of such is the kingdom of God. Verily I say unto you, Whosoever shall not receive the kingdom of God as a little child, he shall not enter therein. *St. Mark* x. 14, 15.

(Cf. *St. Matt.* xix. 14; *St. Luke* xviii. 16, 17.)

The Rich Young Ruler.

The ruler. Good Master, what shall I do to inherit eternal life?

Why callest thou Me good? there is none good

but one, that is, God: but if thou wilt enter into life, keep the commandments.

The ruler.   Which?

Thou shalt do no murder, Thou shalt not commit adultery, Thou shalt not steal, Thou shalt not bear false witness, Honour thy father and thy mother; and, Thou shalt love thy neighbour as thyself.

The ruler.   All these things have I kept, . . . what lack I yet?

If thou wilt be perfect,[1] one thing thou lackest: go thy way, sell whatsoever thou hast, and give to the poor, and thou shalt have treasure in heaven: and come, take up the cross, and follow Me.[2]   [1] *St. Matt.* xix. 17-21; [2] *St. Mark* x. 21.
(Cf. *St. Luke* xviii. 19-22.)

To the Disciples.

How hardly shall they that have riches enter into the kingdom of God!

(*The disciples exceedingly amazed.*)

Children, how hard is it for them that trust in riches to enter into the kingdom of God! It is easier for a camel to go through the eye of a needle, than for a rich man to enter into the kingdom of God.

Disciples.   Who then can be saved?

With men it is impossible, but not with God: for with God all things are possible.

St. Mark x. 23-27.
(Cf. *St. Luke* xviii. 24-27; *St. Matt.* xix. 23-26.)

Peter.   Lo, we have left all, and have followed Thee.

Verily I say unto you, That ye which have followed Me, in the regeneration when the Son of man shall sit in the throne of His glory, ye also shall sit upon twelve thrones, judging the twelve tribes of Israel. *St. Matt.* xix. 28.

Verily I say unto you, There is no man that hath left house, or brethren, or sisters, or father, or mother, or wife, or children, or lands, for My sake, and the gospel's, but he shall receive an hundredfold now in this time, houses, and brethren, and sisters, and mothers, and children, and lands, with persecutions; and in the world to come eternal life. But many that are first shall be last; and the last first. *St. Mark* x. 28-31.
(Cf. *St. Luke* xviii. 29, 30.)

The Labourers in the Vineyard.

For the kingdom of heaven is like unto a man that is an householder, which went out early in the morning to hire labourers into his vineyard. And when he had agreed with the labourers for a penny a day, he sent them into his vineyard. And he went out about the third hour, and saw others standing idle in the marketplace, and said unto them; Go ye also into the vineyard, and whatsoever is right I will give you. And they went their way.

Again he went out about the sixth and ninth hour, and did likewise. And about the eleventh hour he went out, and found others standing idle, and saith unto them, Why stand ye here all the day idle? They say unto him, Because no man hath hired us. He saith unto them, Go ye also into the vineyard; and whatsoever is right, that shall ye receive.

So when even was come, the lord of the vineyard saith unto his steward, Call the labourers, and give them their hire, beginning from the last unto the first. And when they came that were hired about the eleventh hour, they received every man a penny. But when the first came, they supposed that they should have received more; and they likewise received every man a penny. And when they had received it, they murmured against the goodman of the house, saying, These last have wrought but one hour, and thou hast made them equal unto us, which have borne the burden and heat of the day.

But he answered one of them, and said, Friend, I do thee no wrong: didst not thou agree with me for a penny? Take that thine is, and go thy way: I will give unto this last, even as unto thee.

Is it not lawful for me to do what I will with mine own? Is thine eye evil, because I am good?

So the last shall be first, and the first last: for many be called, but few chosen. *St. Matt.* xx. 1–16.

Third Prediction of the Passion.

Behold, we go up to Jerusalem, and all things that are written by the prophets concerning the Son of man shall be accomplished. *St. Luke* xviii. 31.

And the Son of man shall be betrayed unto the chief priests and unto the scribes, and they shall condemn Him to death. *St. Matt.* xx. 18.

For He shall be delivered unto the Gentiles, and shall be mocked, and spitefully entreated, and spitted on: and they shall scourge Him, and put Him to death: and the third day He shall rise again. *St. Luke* xviii. 32, 33.

The Request of James and John.

James and John. Master, ... do for us whatsoever we shall desire.

What would ye that I should do for you?
St. Mark x. 36.

James and John. That we may sit, one on Thy right hand, and the other on Thy left, in Thy kingdom.

Ye know not what ye ask. Are ye able to drink of the cup that I shall drink of, and to be baptized with the baptism that I am baptized with? *St. Matt.* xx. 22.

James and John. We are able.

Ye shall indeed drink of the cup that I drink of; and with the baptism that I am baptized withal shall ye be baptized:[1] but to sit on My right hand, and on My left, is not Mine to give, but it shall be given to them for whom it is prepared of My Father.[2]

[1] *St. Mark* x. 39; [2] *St. Matt.* xx. 23.

To the other Ten Disciples.

Ye know that the princes of the Gentiles exercise dominion over them, and they that are great exercise authority upon them.

But it shall not be so among you: but whosoever will be great among you, let him be your minister; and whosoever will be chief among you, let him be your servant: even as the Son of man came not to be ministered unto, but to minister, and to give His life a ransom for many. *St. Matt.* xx. 25-28.
(Cf. *St. Mark* x. 42-45.)

The Blind Man healed.

AT THE ENTRY TO JERICHO.

What wilt thou that I shall do unto thee?
Blind man. Lord, that I may receive my sight.
Receive thy sight: thy faith hath saved thee.
St. Luke xviii. 41, 42.

The House of Zacchæus.

JERICHO.

Zacchæus, make haste, and come down; for to-day I must abide at thy house.

IN ZACCHÆUS'S HOUSE.

This day is salvation come to this house, forsomuch as he also is a son of Abraham. For the Son of man is come to seek and to save that which was lost. *St. Luke* xix. 5, 9, 10.

Two Blind Men healed.

AT THE GOING OUT FROM JERICHO.

What will ye that I shall do unto you?
Blind men. Lord, that our eyes may be opened.
St. Matt. xx. 32, 33.

To Bartimæus.

What wilt thou that I should do unto thee?
Bartimæus. Lord, that I might receive my sight.
Go thy way; thy faith hath made thee whole.
St. Mark x. 51, 52.

Parable of the Pounds.

NEAR JERUSALEM.

A certain nobleman went into a far country to receive for himself a kingdom, and to return. And he called his ten servants, and delivered them ten pounds, and said unto them, Occupy till I come. But his citizens hated him, and sent a message after him, saying, We will not have this man to reign over us.

And it came to pass, that when he was returned, having received the kingdom, then he commanded these servants to be called unto him, to whom he had given the money, that he might know how much every man had gained by trading.

Then came the first, saying, Lord, thy pound hath gained ten pounds. And he said unto him, Well, thou good servant: because thou hast been faithful in a very little, have thou authority over ten cities. And the second came, saying, Lord, thy pound hath gained five pounds. And he said likewise to him, Be thou also over five cities.

And another came, saying, Lord, behold, here is thy pound, which I have kept laid up in a napkin: for I feared thee, because thou art an austere man: thou takest up that thou layedst not down, and reapest that thou didst not sow.

And he saith unto him, Out of thine own mouth will I judge thee, thou wicked servant. Thou knewest that I was an austere man, taking up that I laid not down, and reaping that I did not sow: wherefore then gavest not thou my money into the bank, that at my coming I might have required mine own with usury?

And he said unto them that stood by, Take from him the pound, and give it to him that hath ten pounds.

(And they said unto him, Lord, he hath ten pounds.)

For I say unto you, That unto every one which hath shall be given; and from him that hath not, even that he hath shall be taken away from him. But those mine enemies, which would not that I should reign over them, bring hither, and slay them before me. *St. Luke* xix. 12–27.

FIFTH PERIOD.
(THE GREAT WEEK.)

From the Supper at Bethany, six days before the Passover, Saturday, April 1 (?), to the Crucifixion, April 7, A.D. 29.

Anointed by Mary in Simon's House, Six Days before the Passover.

BETHANY.

Judas. To what purpose is this waste?

  Let her alone; why trouble ye her? she hath wrought a good work on Me. For ye have the poor with you always, and whensoever ye will ye may do them good: but Me ye have not always. She hath done what she could: she is come aforehand to anoint My body to the burying. Verily I say unto you, Wheresoever this gospel shall be preached throughout the whole world, this also that she hath done shall be spoken of for a memorial of her. *St. Mark* xiv. 6–9.
  (Cf. *St. Matt.* xxvi. 10–13; *St. John* xii. 7, 8.)

THE FIRST DAY OF THE WEEK.
(PALM SUNDAY.)
April 2 (?).

CHIEF EVENTS.

TRIUMPHAL ENTRY INTO JERUSALEM	*St. Mark* xi. 1–10.
JESUS IN THE TEMPLE	*St. Mark* xi. 11.
RETURN TO BETHANY	*St. Mark* xi. 11.

The Procession from Bethany.

To Two Disciples.

Go your way into the village over against you:[1] and as soon as ye be entered into it, ye shall find an ass tied, and a colt with her: loose them, and bring them unto Me.[2] And if any man say unto you, Why do ye this? say ye that the Lord hath need of him; and straightway he will send him hither.[3]

[1] *St. Mark* xi. 2; [2] *St. Matt.* xxi. 2.
[3] *St. Mark* xi. 3.
(Cf. *St. Luke* xix. 30, 31.)

The multitude. Hosanna to the Son of David!
Pharisees. Master, rebuke Thy disciples.

I tell you that, if these should hold their peace, the stones would immediately cry out.

St. Luke xix. 30, 31.

Weeping over Jerusalem.

Mount of Olives.

If thou hadst known, even thou, at least in this thy day, the things which belong unto thy peace! but now they are hid from thine eyes. For the days shall come upon thee, that thine enemies shall cast a trench about thee, and compass thee round, and keep thee in on every side, and shall lay thee even with the ground, and thy children within thee; and they shall not leave in thee one stone upon another; because thou knewest not the time of thy visitation. *St. Luke* xix. 42–44.

SECOND DAY OF THE WEEK.
(MONDAY BEFORE EASTER.)
April 3.
CHIEF EVENTS.

RETURN WITH THE TWELVE EARLY TO JERUSALEM; CURSING
   OF THE BARREN FIG TREE . . . . . *St. Mark* xi. 12–14.
SECOND CLEANSING OF THE TEMPLE . . . *St. Mark* xi. 15–18.
THE CHILDREN'S HOSANNAS . . . . *St. Matt.* xxi. 15, 16.
RETURN TO BETHANY AT EVENING . . . . *St. Mark* xi. 19.

The Cursing of the Fig Tree.

Let no fruit grow on thee henceforward for ever.
St. Matt. xxi. 19.

The Buyers and Sellers driven from the Temple.

Is it not written, My house shall be called of all nations the house of prayer? but ye have made it a den of thieves. *St. Mark* xi. 17.

The Children's Hosannas.

IN THE TEMPLE AT JERUSALEM.

Chief priests and scribes.   Hearest Thou what these say?

Yea; have ye never read, Out of the mouth of babes and sucklings Thou hast perfected praise?
St. Matt. xxi. 16.

THIRD DAY OF THE WEEK.
(TUESDAY BEFORE EASTER.)
April 4.

CHIEF EVENTS.

RETURN TO JERUSALEM IN THE MORNING: THE FIG TREE
    DRIED UP . . . . *St. Mark* xi. 20-26.

JESUS IN THE TEMPLE: HIS AUTHORITY QUESTIONED
                                                     St. Mark xi. 27-33.

THREE PARABLES TO THE PHARISEES
                                    St. Matt. xxi. 28-46; xxii. 1-14.

THREE QUESTIONINGS OF THE HERODIANS, SADDUCEES, AND
    PHARISEES . . . . *St. Matt.* xxii. 15-40.

THE WIDOW'S MITE . . . . *St. Mark* xii. 41-44.

THE VOICE FROM HEAVEN . . . . . *St. John* xii. 28-36.

FINAL DEPARTURE FROM THE TEMPLE . . . . *St. John* xii. 36.

On the Way to the Temple.

Peter. Master, behold, the fig tree which Thou cursedst is withered away.

Have faith in God. For verily I say unto you,[1] If ye have faith, and doubt not, ye shall not only do this which is done to the fig tree, but also [2] whosoever shall say unto this mountain, Be thou removed, and be thou cast into the sea; and shall not doubt in his heart, but shall believe that those things which he saith shall come to pass; he shall have whatsoever he saith. Therefore I say unto you, What things soever ye desire, when ye pray, believe that ye receive them, and ye shall have them.

And when ye stand praying, forgive, if ye have ought against any: that your Father also which is in heaven may forgive you your trespasses. But if ye do not forgive, neither will your Father which is in heaven forgive your trespasses.[3]

[1] *St. Mark* xi. 22; [2] *St. Matt.* xxi. 21;
[3] *St. Mark* xi. 23–26.

THE LAST TEACHING IN THE TEMPLE.

The Question of Authority.

Chief priests and elders. *By what authority doest Thou these things?*

I also will ask you one thing, which if ye tell Me, I in like wise will tell you by what authority I do these things. The baptism of John, whence was it? from heaven, or of men? *St. Matt.* xxi. 24, 25.

Chief priests, etc. *We cannot tell.*

Neither tell I you by what authority I do these things. *St. Matt.* xxi. 27.

Parable of the Two Sons.

But what think ye? A certain man had two sons; and he came to the first, and said, Son, go work to-day in my vineyard. He answered and said, I will not: but afterward he repented, and went. And he came to the second, and said likewise. And he answered and said, I go, sir: and went not.

Whether of them twain did the will of his father?

Chief priests, etc. *The first.*

Verily I say unto you, That the publicans and the harlots go into the kingdom of God before you. For John came unto you in the way of righteousness, and ye believed him not: but the publicans and the harlots believed him: and ye, when ye had seen it, repented not afterward, that ye might believe him. *St. Matt.* xxi. 28–32.

Parable of the Vineyard.

Hear another parable: There was a certain householder, which planted a vineyard, and hedged it round about, and digged a winepress in it, and built a tower,[1] and let it forth to husbandmen, and went into a far country for a long time.[2]

[1] *St. Matt.* xxi. 33; [2] *St. Luke* xx. 9.

And at the season he sent to the husbandmen a servant, that he might receive from the husbandmen of the fruit of the vineyard. And they caught him, and beat him, and sent him away empty. And again he sent unto them another servant; and at him they cast stones, and wounded him in the head, and sent him away shamefully handled. And again he sent another: and him they killed, and many others; beating some, and killing some.

Having yet therefore one son, his well-beloved, he sent him also last unto them, saying, They will reverence my son. But those husbandmen said among themselves, This is the heir; come, let us kill him, and the inheritance shall be ours. And they took him, and killed him, and cast him out of the vineyard.

What shall therefore the lord of the vineyard do? *St. Mark* xii. 2–9.

Chief priests, etc. He will come and destroy the husbandmen, and give the vineyard to others.

Did ye never read in the Scriptures, The stone which the builders rejected, the same is become the head of the corner: this is the Lord's doing, and it is marvellous in our eyes? Therefore say I unto you, The kingdom of God shall be taken from you, and given to a nation bringing forth the fruits thereof. And whosoever shall fall on this stone shall be broken: but on whomsoever it shall fall, it will grind him to powder. *St. Matt.* xxi. 42–44.

Parable of the Marriage Feast.

The kingdom of heaven is like unto a certain king, which made a marriage for his son, and sent forth his servants to call them that were bidden to the wedding: and they would not come.

Again, he sent forth other servants, saying, Tell them which are bidden, Behold, I have prepared my dinner: my oxen and my fatlings are killed, and all things are ready: come unto the marriage. But they made light of it, and went their ways, one to his farm, another to his merchandise: and the remnant took his servants, and entreated them spitefully, and slew them.

But when the king heard thereof, he was wroth: and he sent forth his armies, and destroyed those murderers, and burned up their city. Then saith he to his servants, The wedding is ready, but they which were bidden were not worthy. Go ye therefore into the highways, and as many as ye shall find, bid to the marriage. So those servants went out into the highways, and gathered together all as many as they found, both bad and good: and the wedding was furnished with guests.

And when the king came in to see the guests, he saw there a man which had not on a wedding garment: and he saith unto him, Friend, how camest thou in hither not having a wedding garment? And he was speechless. Then said the king to the servants, Bind him hand and foot, and take him away, and cast him into outer darkness; there shall be weeping and gnashing of teeth.

For many are called, but few are chosen.

St. Matt. xxii. 2-14.

The Question of Tribute.

Pharisees and Herodians. Is it lawful to give tribute unto Cæsar, or not?

Why tempt ye Me, ye hypocrites? Show Me the tribute money.

(*They brought it.*)

Whose is this image and superscription?

Pharisees, etc. Cæsar's.

Render therefore unto Cæsar the things which are Cæsar's; and unto God the things that are God's. *St. Matt.* xxii. 18-21.

(Cf. *St. Mark* xii. 14-17; *St. Luke* xx. 21-25.)

The Question of the Resurrection.

Sadducees. Whose wife shall she be of the seven? for they all had her.

Do ye not therefore err, because ye know not the Scriptures, neither the power of God?

St. Mark xii. 24.

The children of this world marry, and are given in marriage: but they which shall be accounted worthy to obtain that world, and the resurrection from the dead, neither marry, nor are given in marriage: neither can they die any more: for they are equal unto the angels; and are the children of God, being the children of the resurrection.

Now that the dead are raised, even Moses showed at the bush, when he calleth the Lord the God of Abraham, and the God of Isaac, and the God of Jacob. For He is not a God of the dead, but of the living: for all live unto Him.

St. Luke xx. 34–38.
(Cf. *St. Matt.* xxii. 29–32; *St. Mark* xii. 24–27.)

The Lawyer's Question.

Lawyer. Which is the first commandment of all?

The first of all the commandments is, Hear, O Israel; The Lord our God is one Lord: and thou shalt love the Lord thy God with all thy heart, and with all thy soul, and with all thy mind, and with all thy strength: this is the first commandment. And the second is like, namely this, Thou shalt love thy neighbour as thyself. There is none other commandment greater than these.

St. Mark xii. 29–31.
(Cf. *St. Matt.* xxii. 37–39.)

On these two commandments hang all the Law and the prophets. *St. Matt.* xxii. 40.

Lawyer. Well, Master, Thou hast said the truth.

Thou art not far from the kingdom of God.

St. Mark xii. 34.

Our Lord's Question.

To the Pharisees.

What think ye of Christ? whose Son is He?

St. Matt. xxii. 42.

Pharisees.   The Son of David.

How say the scribes that Christ is the Son of David? For David himself said by the Holy Ghost, The Lord said to my Lord, Sit Thou on My right hand, till I make Thine enemies Thy footstool. David therefore himself calleth Him Lord; and whence is He then his Son?

St. Mark xii. 35-37.

To the Multitude, and to the Disciples.

Beware of the scribes, which love to go in long clothing, and love salutations in the marketplaces.

St. Mark xii. 38.

The scribes and the Pharisees sit in Moses' seat: all therefore whatsoever they bid you observe, that observe and do; but do not ye after their works: for they say, and do not. For they bind heavy burdens and grievous to be borne, and lay them on men's shoulders; but they themselves will not move them with one of their fingers. But all their works they do for to be seen of men: they make broad their phylacteries, and enlarge the borders of their garments, and love the uppermost rooms at feasts, and the chief seats in the synagogues, and greetings in the markets, and to be called of men, Rabbi, Rabbi.

But be not ye called Rabbi: for One is your Master, even Christ; and all ye are brethren. And call no man your father upon the earth: for One is your Father, which is in heaven. Neither be ye called masters: for One is your Master, even Christ. But he that is greatest among you shall be your servant. And whosoever shall exalt himself shall be abased; and he that shall humble himself shall be exalted.

St. Matt. xxiii. 2-12.

The Woes denounced in the Temple.

But woe unto you, scribes and Pharisees, hypocrites! for ye shut up the kingdom of heaven against men: for ye neither go in yourselves, neither suffer ye them that are entering to go in.

Woe unto you, scribes and Pharisees, hypocrites! for ye devour widows' houses, and for a pretence make long prayer: therefore ye shall receive the greater damnation.

Woe unto you, scribes and Pharisees, hypocrites! for ye compass sea and land to make one proselyte, and when he is made, ye make him twofold more the child of hell than yourselves.

Woe unto you, ye blind guides, which say, Whosoever shall swear by the temple, it is nothing; but whosoever shall swear by the gold of the temple, he is a debtor! Ye fools and blind: for whether is greater, the gold, or the temple that sanctifieth the gold? And, Whosoever shall swear by the altar, it is nothing; but whosoever sweareth by the gift that is upon it, he is guilty. Ye fools and blind: for whether is greater, the gift, or the altar that sanctifieth the gift? Whoso therefore shall swear by the altar, sweareth by it, and by all things thereon. And whoso shall swear by the temple, sweareth by it, and by him that dwelleth therein. And he that shall swear by heaven, sweareth by the throne of God, and by Him that sitteth thereon.

Woe unto you, scribes and Pharisees, hypocrites! for ye pay tithe of mint and anise and cummin, and have omitted the weightier matters of the Law, judgment, mercy, and faith: these ought ye to have done, and not to leave the other undone. Ye blind guides, which strain at a gnat, and swallow a camel.

Woe unto you, scribes and Pharisees, hypocrites! for ye make clean the outside of the cup and of the platter, but within they are full of extortion and excess. Thou blind Pharisee, cleanse first that which is within the cup and platter, that the outside of them may be clean also.

Woe unto you, scribes and Pharisees, hypocrites! for ye are like unto whited sepulchres, which indeed appear beautiful outward, but are within full of dead men's bones, and of all uncleanness. Even so ye also outwardly appear righteous unto men, but within ye are full of hypocrisy and iniquity.

Woe unto you, scribes and Pharisees, hypocrites! because ye build the tombs of the prophets, and garnish the sepulchres of the righteous, and say, If we had been in the days of our fathers, we would not have been partakers with them in the blood of the prophets. Wherefore ye be witnesses unto yourselves, that ye are the children of them which killed the prophets. Fill ye up then the measure of your fathers. Ye serpents, ye generation of vipers, how can ye escape the damnation of hell?

Wherefore, behold, I send unto you prophets, and wise men, and scribes: and some of them ye shall kill and crucify; and some of them shall ye scourge in your synagogues, and persecute them from city to city: that upon you may come all the righteous blood shed upon the earth, from the blood of righteous Abel unto the blood of Zacharias son of Barachias, whom ye slew between the temple and the altar. Verily I say unto you, All these things shall come upon this generation.

O Jerusalem, Jerusalem, thou that killest the prophets, and stonest them which are sent unto thee, how often would I have gathered thy children together, even as a hen gathereth her chickens under her wing, and ye would not!

Behold, your house is left unto you desolate. For I say unto you, Ye shall not see Me henceforth, till ye shall say, Blessed is He that cometh in the Name of the Lord! *St. Matt.* xxiii. 13-39. (Cf. *St. Mark* xii. 40.)

The Widow's Two Mites.
AT THE TREASURY IN THE TEMPLE.

To the Disciples.

Verily I say unto you, That this poor widow hath cast more in, than all they which have cast into the treasury. *St. Mark* xii. 43.

For all these have of their abundance cast in unto the offerings of God: but she of her penury hath cast in all the living that she had. *St. Luke* xxi. 4.

The Greeks brought to Christ.

Greeks. We would see Jesus.

The hour is come that the Son of man should be glorified. Verily, verily, I say unto you, Except a corn of wheat fall into the ground and die, it abideth alone: but if it die, it bringeth forth much fruit. He that loveth his life shall lose it; and he that hateth his life in this world shall keep it unto life eternal.

If any man serve Me, let him follow Me; and where I am, there shall also My servant be: if any man serve Me, him will My Father honour. Now is My soul troubled; and what shall I say? Father, save Me from this hour: but for this cause came I unto this hour. Father, glorify Thy Name.
St. John xii. 23-28.

The Voice from heaven. I HAVE BOTH GLORIFIED IT, AND WILL GLORIFY IT AGAIN.

This voice came not because of Me, but for your sakes. Now is the judgment of this world: now shall the prince of this world be cast out. And I, if I be lifted up from the earth, will draw all men unto Me.
St. John xii. 30-32.

The people. How sayest Thou, The Son of man must be lifted up?

Yet a little while is the light with you. Walk while ye have the light, lest darkness come upon you: for he that walketh in darkness knoweth not whither he goeth. While ye have light, believe in the light, that ye may be the children of light.
St. John xii. 35, 36.

Unbelief of the Jews.

He that believeth on Me, believeth not on Me, but on Him that sent Me. And he that seeth Me seeth Him that sent Me.

I am come a Light into the world, that whosoever believeth on Me should not abide in darkness. And if any man hear My words, and believe not, I judge him not: for I came not to judge the world, but to save the world. He that rejecteth Me, and receiveth not My words, hath one that judgeth him : the word that I have spoken, the same shall judge him in the last day. For I have not spoken of Myself; but the Father which sent Me, He gave Me a commandment, what I should say, and what I should speak. And I know that His commandment is life everlasting: whatsoever I speak therefore, even as the Father said unto Me, so I speak. *St. John* xii. 44-50.

Jesus departs from the Temple.

One of the disciples. Master, see . . . what buildings are here.

Seest thou these great buildings? *St. Mark* xiii. 2.

As for these things which ye behold, the days will come, in the which there shall not be left one stone upon another, that shall not be thrown down. *St. Luke* xxi. 6.

FOURTH DAY OF THE WEEK.
(WEDNESDAY BEFORE EASTER.)[1]

April 5.

ON THE MOUNT OF OLIVES.

PROPHECY OF DESTRUCTION OF JERUSALEM	*St. Matt.* xxiv. 3–51.
THE THREE LAST PARABLES	*St. Matt.* xxv.
UNBELIEF OF THE JEWS	*St. John* xii. 37–50.
JUDAS SELLS HIS MASTER	*St. Luke* xxii. 3–6.

[1] The discourse on the Mount of Olives is by many supposed to have been on the evening of Tuesday.

Discourse on the Mount of Olives.

Disciples. Master, but when shall these things be?

Take heed that no man deceive you. For many shall come in My Name, saying, I am Christ; and shall deceive many. And ye shall hear of wars and rumours of wars: see that ye be not troubled: for all these things must come to pass, but the end is not yet. For nation shall rise against nation, and kingdom against kingdom: and there shall be famines, and pestilences, and earthquakes, in divers places. *St. Matt.* xxiv. 4–7.

And fearful sights and great signs shall there be from heaven. *St. Luke* xxi. 11.

All these are the beginning of sorrows.
St. Matt. xxiv. 8.

(Cf. *St. Mark* xiii. 5–8; *St. Luke* xxi. 8–11.)

But take heed to yourselves:[1] before all these, they shall lay their hands on you, and persecute you, delivering you up to the synagogues, and into prisons,[2] and in the synagogues ye shall be beaten: and ye shall be brought before rulers and kings for My sake, for a testimony against them. And the gospel must first be published among all nations.[3]   [1] *St. Mark* xiii. 9; [2] *St. Luke* xxi. 12;
[3] *St. Mark* xiii. 9, 10.

But when they shall lead you, and deliver you up, take no thought beforehand what ye shall speak, neither do ye premeditate: but whatsoever shall be given you in that hour, that speak ye: for it is not ye that speak, but the Holy Ghost.
St. Mark xiii. 11.

For I will give you a mouth and wisdom, which all your adversaries shall not be able to gainsay or resist. *St. Luke* xxi. 15.

Now the brother shall betray the brother to death, and the father the son; and children shall rise up against their parents, and shall cause them to be put to death. And ye shall be hated of all men for My Name's sake. *St. Mark* xiii. 12, 13.

But there shall not an hair of your head perish.
St. Luke xxi. 18.

And many false prophets shall rise, and shall deceive many. And because iniquity shall abound, the love of many shall wax cold. But he that shall endure unto the end, the same shall be saved.
St. Matt. xxiv. 11–13.

In your patience possess ye your souls.
St. Luke xxi. 18.

And this gospel of the kingdom shall be preached in all the world for a witness unto all nations; and then shall the end come. When ye therefore shall see the abomination of desolation, spoken of by Daniel the prophet, stand in the holy place, (whoso readeth, let him understand:) then let them which be in Judæa flee into the mountains: let him which is on the housetop not come down to take anything out of his house: neither let him which is in the field return back to take his clothes. *St. Matt.* xxiv. 14–18.

(Cf. *St. Mark* xiii. 14–16; *St. Luke* xxi. 20, 21.)

For these be the days of vengeance, that all things which are written may be fulfilled.

St. Luke xxi. 22.

And woe unto them that are with child, and to them that give suck in those days! But pray ye that your flight be not in the winter, neither on the sabbath day: for then shall be great tribulation, such as was not since the beginning of the world to this time, no, nor ever shall be.

St. Matt. xxiv. 19–21.

(Cf. *St. Mark* xiii. 17–19; *St. Luke* xxi. 23.)

And they shall fall by the edge of the sword, and shall be led away captive into all nations: and Jerusalem shall be trodden down of the Gentiles, until the times of the Gentiles be fulfilled.

St. Luke xxi. 24.

And except those days should be shortened, there should no flesh be saved: but for the elect's sake those days shall be shortened.

Then if any man shall say unto you, Lo, here is Christ, or there; believe it not. For there shall arise false Christs, and false prophets, and shall show great signs and wonders; insomuch that, if it were possible, they shall deceive the very elect.

Behold, I have told you before. Wherefore if they shall say unto you, Behold, he is in the desert; go not forth: behold, he is in the secret chambers; believe it not. For as the lightning cometh out of the east, and shineth even unto the west; so shall also the coming of the Son of man be. For wheresoever the carcase is, there will the eagles be gathered together.

Immediately after the tribulation of those days shall the sun be darkened, and the moon shall not give her light, and the stars shall fall from heaven,[1] and upon the earth distress of nations, with perplexity; the sea and the waves roaring; men's hearts failing them for fear, and for looking after those things which are coming on the earth: for the powers of heaven shall be shaken.[2]

[1] *St. Matt.* xxiv. 22-29; [2] *St. Luke* xxi. 25, 26. (Cf. *St. Mark* xiii. 24, 25.)

And then shall appear the sign of the Son of man in heaven: and then shall all the tribes of the earth mourn, and they shall see the Son of man coming in the clouds of heaven with power and great glory. And He shall send His angels with a great sound of a trumpet, and they shall gather together His elect from the four winds, from one end of heaven to the other. *St. Matt.* xxiv. 30, 31.

(Cf. *St. Mark* xiii. 26, 27; *St. Luke* xxi. 27.)

And when these things begin to come to pass, then look up, and lift up your heads; for your redemption draweth nigh. *St. Luke* xxi. 28.

Now learn a parable of the fig tree; When her branch is yet tender, and putteth forth leaves, ye know that summer is near: so ye in like manner, when ye shall see these things come to pass, know that it is nigh, even at the doors.

Verily I say unto you, that this generation shall not pass, till all these things be done. Heaven and earth shall pass away: but My words shall not pass away.

But of that day and that hour knoweth no man, no, not the angels which are in heaven, neither the Son, but the Father. *St. Mark* xiii. 28-32.

(Cf. *St. Matt.* xxiv. 32-36; *St. Luke* xxi. 29-33.)

But as the days of Noe were, so shall also the coming of the Son of man be. For as in the days that were before the flood they were eating and drinking, marrying and giving in marriage, until the day that Noe entered into the ark, and knew not until the flood came, and took them all away; so shall also the coming of the Son of man be.

Then shall two be in the field; the one shall be taken, and the other left. Two women shall be grinding at the mill; the one shall be taken, and the other left. *St. Matt.* xxiv. 37–41

And take heed to yourselves, lest at any time your hearts be overcharged with surfeiting, and drunkenness, and cares of this life, and so that day come upon you unawares. For as a snare shall it come on all them that dwell on the face of the whole earth.

Watch ye therefore, and pray always, that ye may be accounted worthy to escape all these things that shall come to pass, and to stand before the Son of man. *St. Luke* xxi. 34–36.

Watch therefore: for ye know not what hour your Lord doth come. But know this, that if the goodman of the house had known in what watch the thief would come, he would have watched, and would not have suffered his house to be broken up. Therefore be ye also ready: for in such an hour as ye think not the Son of man cometh.

Who then is a faithful and wise servant, whom his lord hath made ruler over his household, to give them meat in due season? Blessed is that servant, whom his lord when he cometh shall find so doing. Verily I say unto you, That he shall make him ruler over all his goods.

But and if that evil servant shall say in his heart, My lord delayeth his coming; and shall begin to smite his fellow-servants, and to eat and drink with the drunken; the lord of that servant shall come in a day when he looketh not for him, and in an hour that he is not aware of, and shall cut him asunder, and appoint him his portion with the hypocrites: there shall be weeping and gnashing of teeth. *St. Matt.* xxiv. 42–51.

Take ye heed, watch and pray: for ye know not when the time is. For the Son of man is as a man taking a far journey, who left his house, and gave authority to his servants, and to every man his work, and commanded the porter to watch.

Watch ye therefore: for ye know not when the Master of the house cometh, at even, or at midnight, or at the cockcrowing, or in the morning: lest coming suddenly He find you sleeping.

And what I say unto you I say unto all, Watch.
St. Mark xiii. 33–37.

THE THREE LAST GREAT PARABLES.

On the Mount of Olives.

The Ten Virgins.[1]

To the Disciples.

Then shall the kingdom of heaven be likened unto ten virgins, which took their lamps, and went forth to meet the bridegroom. And five of them were wise, and five were foolish.

They that were foolish took their lamps, and took no oil with them: but the wise took oil in their vessels with their lamps.

[1] For those especially who embrace counsels of perfection.

While the bridegroom tarried, they all slumbered and slept. And at midnight there was a cry made, Behold, the bridegroom cometh; go ye out to meet him.

Then all those virgins arose, and trimmed their lamps. And the foolish said unto the wise, Give us of your oil; for our lamps are gone out. But the wise answered, saying, Not so; lest there be not enough for us and you: but go ye rather to them that sell, and buy for yourselves.

And while they went to buy, the bridegroom came; and they that were ready went in with him to the marriage: and the door was shut. Afterward came also the other virgins, saying, Lord, Lord, open to us. But he answered and said, Verily I say unto you, I know you not.

Watch therefore, for ye know neither the day nor the hour wherein the Son of man cometh.

St. Matt. xxv. 1–13.

The Talents.[1]

For the kingdom of heaven is as a man travelling into a far country, who called his own servants, and delivered unto them his goods. And unto one he gave five talents, to another two, and to another one; to every man according to his several ability; and straightway took his journey. Then he that had received the five talents went and traded with the same, and made them other five talents. And likewise he that had received two, he also gained other two. But he that had

---

[1] For all Christians.

received one went and digged in the earth, and hid his lord's money.

After a long time the lord of those servants cometh, and reckoneth with them. And so he that had received five talents came and brought other five talents, saying, Lord, thou deliveredst unto me five talents: behold, I have gained beside them five talents more. His lord said unto him, Well done, thou good and faithful servant: thou hast been faithful over a few things, I will make thee ruler over many things: enter thou into the joy of thy lord.

He also that had received two talents came and said, Lord, thou deliveredst unto me two talents: behold, I have gained two other talents beside them. His lord said unto him, Well done, good and faithful servant; thou hast been faithful over a few things, I will make thee ruler over many things: enter thou into the joy of thy lord. Then he which had received the one talent came and said, Lord, I knew thee that thou art an hard man, reaping where thou hast not sown, and gathering where thou hast not strawed: and I was afraid, and went and hid thy talent in the earth: lo, there thou hast that is thine.

His lord answered and said unto him, Thou wicked and slothful servant, thou knewest that I reap where I sowed not, and gather where I have not strawed: thou oughtest therefore to have put my money to the exchangers, and then at my coming I should have received mine own with usury. Take therefore the talent from him, and give it unto him which hath ten talents. For unto every one that hath shall be given, and he shall have abundance: but from him that hath not shall be taken away even that which he hath. And cast ye the unprofitable servant into outer darkness: there shall be weeping and gnashing of teeth. *St. Matt.* xxv. 14–30.

The Sheep and the Goats.[1]

When the Son of man shall come in His glory, and all the holy angels with Him, then shall He sit upon the throne of His glory: and before Him shall be gathered all nations: and He shall separate them one from another, as a shepherd divideth his sheep from the goats: and He shall set the sheep on His right hand, but the goats on the left.

Then shall the King say unto them on His right hand, Come, ye blessed of My Father, inherit the kingdom prepared for you from the foundation of the world: for I was an hungred, and ye gave Me meat: I was thirsty, and ye gave Me drink: I was a stranger, and ye took Me in: naked, and ye clothed Me: I was sick, and ye visited Me: I was in prison, and ye came unto Me.

Then shall the righteous answer Him, saying, Lord, when saw we Thee an hungred, and fed Thee? or thirsty, and gave Thee drink? When saw we Thee a stranger, and took Thee in? or naked, and clothed Thee? Or when saw we Thee sick, or in prison, and came unto Thee? And the King shall answer and say unto them, Verily I say unto you, Inasmuch as ye have done

[1] For all men.

it unto one of the least of these My brethren, ye have done it unto Me.

Then shall He say also unto them on the left hand, Depart from Me, ye cursed, into everlasting fire, prepared for the devil and his angels: for I was an hungred, and ye gave Me no meat: I was thirsty, and ye gave Me no drink: I was a stranger, and ye took Me not in: naked, and ye clothed Me not: sick, and in prison, and ye visited Me not.

Then shall they also answer Him, saying, Lord, when saw we Thee an hungred, or athirst, or a stranger, or naked, or sick, or in prison, and did not minister unto Thee? Then shall He answer them, saying, Verily I say unto you, Inasmuch as ye did it not to one of the least of these, ye did it not to Me. And these shall go away into everlasting punishment: but the righteous into life eternal. *St. Matt.* xxv. 31–46.

Preparation for the Passover.

To the Disciples.

Ye know that after two days is the Feast of the Passover, and the Son of man is betrayed to be crucified. *St. Matt.* xxvi. 2.

FIFTH DAY OF THE WEEK.
(MAUNDY THURSDAY.)
April 6.

CHIEF EVENTS.

DISCIPLES SENT TO PREPARE THE PASSOVER   *St. Mark* xiv. 12–16.
THE LAST SUPPER . . . . *St. Luke* xxii. 14–18.
WASHING THE DISCIPLES' FEET   . . .   . *St. John* xiii. 2–17.
BETRAYAL OF JUDAS DECLARED: HE GOES OUT *St. John* xiii. 18–30.
INSTITUTION OF THE EUCHARIST . .   . *St. Matt.* xxvi. 26–29.
LAST DISCOURSES: PROMISE OF THE COMFORTER
                    St. John xiii. 31–38 ; xiv., xv., xvi.
THE GREAT INTERCESSION .   . . *St. John* xvii.
THE AGONY AT GETHSEMANE
                St. Mark xiv. 32–42 ; *St. Luke* xxii. 43–46.
JESUS TAKEN PRISONER .   . . . . . *St. John* xviii. 1–12.
BROUGHT BEFORE ANNAS . .   .   . . *St. John* xviii. 13.
ACCUSED BEFORE CAIAPHAS, AND MOCKED   *St. Matt.* xxvi. 57–68.
DENIED BY ST. PETER . . . . *St. Matt.* xxvi. 69–75.

Preparation of the Passover.

To Peter and John.

Go and prepare us the Passover, that we may eat. *St. Luke* xxii. 8.

Disciples. Where wilt Thou that we prepare?

Go ye into the city, and there shall meet you a man bearing a pitcher of water: follow him. And wheresoever he shall go in, say ye to the goodman of the house, The Master saith, Where is the guest-chamber, where I shall eat the Passover with My disciples? And he will show you a large upper room furnished and prepared: there make ready for us. *St. Mark* xiv. 13-15.
(Cf. *St. Matt.* xxvi. 18; *St. Luke* xxii. 10, 11.)

The Last Supper.

THE UPPER ROOM AT JERUSALEM.

To the Disciples.

With desire I have desired to eat this Passover with you before I suffer: for I say unto you, I will not any more eat thereof, until it be fulfilled in the kingdom of God. And He took the cup, and gave thanks, and said, Take this, and divide it among yourselves: for I say unto you, I will not drink of the fruit of the vine, until the kingdom of God shall come. *St. Luke* xxii. 15–18.

Washing the Disciples' Feet.

Peter. *Lord, dost Thou wash my feet?*

What I do thou knowest not now; but thou shalt know hereafter.

Peter. *Thou shalt never wash my feet.*

If I wash thee not, thou hast no part with Me.

Peter. *Lord, not my feet only, but also my hands and my head.*

He that is washed needeth not save to wash his feet, but is clean every whit: and ye are clean, but not all.

(*When He was set down again.*)

Know ye what I have done to you? Ye call Me Master and Lord: and ye say well; for so I am. If I then, your Lord and Master, have washed your feet; ye also ought to wash one another's feet.

For I have given you an example, that ye should do as I have done to you. Verily, verily, I say unto you, The servant is not greater than his lord; neither he that is sent greater than He that sent him. If ye know these things, happy are ye if ye do them. *St. John* xiii. 7–17.

(*Disciples dispute as to which should be greatest.*)

The kings of the Gentiles exercise lordship over them; and they that exercise authority upon them are called benefactors. But ye shall not be so: but he that is greatest among you, let him be as the younger; and he that is chief, as he that doth serve. For whether is greater, he that sitteth at meat, or he that serveth? is not he that sitteth at meat? but I am among you as He that serveth. Ye are they which have continued with Me in My temptations. And I appoint unto you a kingdom, as My Father hath appointed unto Me; that ye may eat and drink at My table in My kingdom, and sit on thrones judging the twelve tribes of Israel. *St. Luke* xxii. 25–30.

I speak not of you all: I know whom I have chosen: but that the Scripture may be fulfilled, He that eateth bread with Me hath lifted up his heel against Me. Now I tell you before it come, that, when it is come to pass, ye may believe that I am He. Verily, verily, I say unto you, He that receiveth whomsoever I send receiveth Me; and he that receiveth Me receiveth Him that sent Me. *St. John* xiii. 18–20.

Judas's Treachery declared.

Verily I say unto you, One of you which eateth with Me shall betray Me. *St. Mark* xiv. 18.
(Cf. *St. Matt.* xxvi. 21; *St. John* xiii. 21.)

Disciples. Is it I? Is it I?

It is one of the twelve, that dippeth with Me in the dish. The Son of man indeed goeth, as it is written of Him: but woe to that man by whom the Son of man is betrayed! good were it for that man if he had never been born. *St. Mark* xiv. 20, 21.

John. *Lord, who is it?*

He it is, to whom I shall give a sop, when I have dipped it. *St. John* xiii. 26

(Cf. *St. Matt.* xxvi. 25)

Judas. *Master, is it I?*

Thou hast said. *St. Matt.* xxvi. 25.

(*The sop given to Judas.*)

That thou doest, do quickly. *St. John* xiii. 27.

St. Peter warned.

Now is the Son of man glorified, and God is glorified in Him. If God be glorified in Him, God shall also glorify Him in Himself, and shall straightway glorify Him.

Little children, yet a little while I am with you. Ye shall seek Me: and as I said unto the Jews, Whither I go, ye cannot come; so now I say to you. A new commandment I give unto you, That ye love one another; as I have loved you, that ye also love one another. By this shall all men know that ye are My disciples, if ye have love one to another. *St. John* xiii. 31–35.

Peter. *Lord, whither goest Thou?*

Whither I go, Thou canst not follow Me now; but thou shalt follow Me afterwards.[1] Simon, Simon, behold, Satan hath desired to have you, that he may sift you as wheat: but I have prayed for thee, that thy faith fail not: and when thou art converted, strengthen thy brethren.[2]

[1] *St. John* xiii. 36; [2] *St. Luke* xxii. 31, 32.

Peter. Why cannot I follow Thee now? I will lay down my life for Thy sake.

Wilt thou lay down thy life for My sake? Verily, verily, I say unto thee, The cock shall not crow, till thou hast denied Me thrice. *St. John* xiii. 38.
(Cf. *St. Luke* xxii. 34.)

When I sent you without purse, and scrip, and shoes, lacked ye anything?

Disciples. Nothing.

But now, he that hath a purse, let him take it, and likewise his scrip: and he that hath no sword, let him sell his garment, and buy one. For I say unto you, that this that is written must yet be accomplished in Me, And He was reckoned among the transgressors: for the things concerning Me have an end.

Disciples. Lord, behold here are two swords.

It is enough. *St. Luke* xxii. 35-38.

Institution of the Eucharist.

(*Our Lord takes bread, blesses, breaks it, and gives it unto the disciples.*)

Take, eat; THIS IS MY BODY,[1] WHICH IS GIVEN FOR YOU: this do in remembrance of Me.[2]

[1] *St. Matt.* xxvi. 26; [2] *St. Luke* xxii. 19.
(Cf. *St. Mark* xiv. 22; 1 *Cor.* xi. 24.)

(*He takes the cup and gives thanks.*)

Drink ye all of it; for THIS IS MY BLOOD OF THE NEW TESTAMENT, which is shed for many for the remission of sins.[1] This do ye, as oft as ye drink it, in remembrance of Me.[2]

[1] *St. Matt.* xxvi. 28; [2] 1 Cor. xi. 25.
(Cf. *St. Mark* xiv. 24; *St. Luke* xxii. 20.)

But I say unto you, I will not drink henceforth of this fruit of the vine, until that day when I drink it new with you in My Father's kingdom.

St. Matt. xxvi. 29.

Let not your heart be troubled: ye believe in God, believe also in Me. In My Father's house are many mansions: if it were not so, I would have told you. I go to prepare a place for you. And if I go and prepare a place for you, I will come again, and receive you unto Myself; that where I am, there ye may be also. And whither I go ye know, and the way ye know.

Thomas. Lord . . . how can we know the way?

I am the Way, the Truth, and the Life: no man cometh unto the Father, but by Me. If ye had known Me, ye should have known My Father also: and from henceforth ye know Him, and have seen Him.

Philip. Lord, show us the Father.

Have I been so long time with you, and yet hast thou not known Me, Philip? he that hath seen Me hath seen the Father; and how sayest thou then, Show us the Father? Believest thou not that I am in the Father, and the Father in Me? the words that I speak unto you I speak not of Myself: but the Father that dwelleth in Me, He doeth the works. Believe Me that I am in the Father, and the Father in Me: or else believe Me for the very works' sake.

Verily, verily, I say unto you, He that believeth on Me, the works that I do shall he do also; and greater works than these shall he do; because I go unto My Father. And whatsoever ye shall ask in My Name, that will I do, that the Father may be glorified in the Son. If ye shall ask anything in My Name, I will do it.

If ye love Me, keep My commandments. And I will pray the Father, and He shall give you another Comforter, that He may abide with you for ever; even the Spirit of Truth; whom the world cannot receive, because it seeth Him not, neither knoweth Him: but ye know Him; for He dwelleth with you, and shall be in you. I will not leave you comfortless: I will come to you.

Yet a little while, and the world seeth Me no more; but ye see Me: because I live, ye shall live also. At that day ye shall know that I am in My Father, and ye in Me, and I in you. He that hath My commandments, and keepeth them, he it is that loveth Me: and he that loveth Me shall be loved of My Father, and I will love him, and will manifest Myself to him.

Jude. *Lord, how is it that Thou wilt manifest Thyself unto us?*

If a man love Me, he will keep My words: and My Father will love him, and we will come unto him, and make our abode with him. He that loveth Me not keepeth not My sayings: and the word which ye hear is not Mine, but the Father's which sent Me.

These things have I spoken unto you, being yet present with you. But the Comforter, which is the Holy Ghost, whom the Father will send in My Name, He shall teach you all things, and bring all things to your remembrance, whatsoever I have said unto you.

Peace I leave with you, My peace I give unto you: not as the world giveth, give I unto you.

Let not your heart be troubled, neither let it be afraid. Ye have heard how I said unto you, I go away, and come again unto you. If ye loved Me, ye would rejoice, because I said, I go unto the Father: for My Father is greater than I. And now I have told you before it come to pass, that, when it is come to pass, ye might believe.

Hereafter I will not talk much with you: for the prince of this world cometh, and hath nothing in Me. But that the world may know that I love the Father: and as the Father gave me commandment, even so I do. Arise, let us go hence.

St. John xiv.

The True Vine.

On the Way to the Garden of the Agony (?).

I am the true Vine, and My Father is the Husbandman. Every branch in Me that beareth not fruit He taketh away: and every branch that beareth fruit, He purgeth it, that it may bring forth more fruit. Now ye are clean through the word which I have spoken unto you. Abide in Me, and I in you. As the branch cannot bear fruit of itself, except it abide in the vine; no more can ye, except ye abide in Me. I am the Vine, ye are the branches: he that abideth in Me, and I in him, the same bringeth forth much fruit: for without Me ye can do nothing. If a man abide not in Me, he is cast forth as a branch, and is withered; and men gather them, and cast them into the fire, and they are burned. If ye abide in Me, and My words abide in you, ye shall ask what ye will, and it shall be done unto you. Herein is My Father glorified, that ye bear much fruit; so shall ye be My disciples.

As the Father hath loved Me, so have I loved you: continue ye in My love. If ye keep My commandments, ye shall abide in My love; even as I have kept My Father's commandments, and abide in His love. These things have I spoken unto you, that My joy might remain in you, and that your joy might be full. This is My commandment, That ye love one another, as I have loved you. Greater love hath no man than this, that a man lay down his life for his friends.

Ye are My friends, if ye do whatsoever I command you. Henceforth I call you not servants; for the servant knoweth not what his lord doeth: but I have called you friends; for all things that I have heard of My Father I have made known unto you. Ye have not chosen Me, but I have chosen you, and ordained you, that ye should go and bring forth fruit, and that your fruit should remain: that whatsoever ye shall ask of the Father in My Name, He may give it you. These things I command you, that ye love one another.

If the world hate you, ye know that it hated Me before it hated you. If ye were of the world, the world would love his own: but because ye are not of the world, but I have chosen you out of the world, therefore the world hateth you. Remember the word that I said unto you, The servant is not greater than his lord. If they have persecuted Me, they will also persecute you; if they have kept My saying, they will keep yours also. But all these things will they do unto you for My Name's sake, because they know not Him that sent Me. If I had not come and spoken unto them, they had not had sin: but now they have no cloke for their sin.

He that hateth Me hateth My Father also. If I had not done among them the works which none other man did, they had not had sin: but now have they both seen and hated both Me and My Father. But this cometh to pass, that the word might be fulfilled that is written in their Law, They hated Me without a cause.

But when the Comforter is come, whom I will send unto you from the Father, even the Spirit of Truth, which proceedeth from the Father, He shall testify of Me: and ye also shall bear witness, because ye have been with Me from the beginning.

St. John xv.

Promise of the Comforter.

These things have I spoken unto you, that ye should not be offended. They shall put you out of the synagogues: yea, the time cometh, that whosoever killeth you will think that he doeth God service. And these things will they do unto you, because they have not known the Father, nor Me. But these things have I told you, that when the time shall come, ye may remember that I told you of them. And these things I said not unto you at the beginning, because I was with you. But now I go My way to Him that sent Me; and none of you asketh Me, Whither goest Thou? But because I have said these things unto you, sorrow hath filled your heart.

Nevertheless I tell you the truth; It is expedient for you that I go away : for if I go not away, the Comforter will not come unto you; but if I depart, I will send Him unto you. And when He is come, He will reprove the world of sin, and of righteousness, and of judgment :

Of sin, because they believe not on Me; of righteousness, because I go to My Father, and ye see Me no more; of judgment, because the prince of this world is judged.

I have yet many things to say unto you, but ye cannot bear them now. Howbeit when He, the Spirit of Truth, is come, He will guide you into all truth : for He shall not speak of Himself; but whatsoever He shall hear, that shall He speak : and He will show you things to come. He shall glorify Me; for He shall receive of Mine, and shall show it unto you. All things that the Father hath are Mine : therefore said I, that He shall take of Mine, and shall show it unto you. A little while, and ye shall not see Me : and again, a little while, and ye shall see Me, because I go to the Father. *St. John* xvi. 1–16.

Some disciples. A little while? We cannot tell what He saith.

Do ye inquire among yourselves of that I said, A little while, and ye shall not see Me : and again, a little while, and ye shall see Me? Verily, verily, I say unto you, That ye shall weep and lament, but the world shall rejoice : and ye shall be sorrowful, but your sorrow shall be turned into joy. A woman when she is in travail hath sorrow, because her hour is come : but as soon as she is delivered of the child, she remembereth no more the anguish, for joy that a man is born into the world. And ye now therefore have sorrow: but I will see you again, and your heart shall rejoice, and your joy no man taketh from you.

And in that day ye shall ask Me nothing. Verily, verily, I say unto you, Whatsoever ye shall ask the Father in My Name, He will give it you. Hitherto have ye asked nothing in My Name: ask, and ye shall receive, that your joy may be full.

These things have I spoken unto you in proverbs: but the time cometh, when I shall no more speak unto you in proverbs, but I shall show you plainly of the Father. At that day ye shall ask in My Name: and I say not unto you, that I will pray the Father for you: for the Father Himself loveth you, because ye have loved Me, and have believed that I came out from God.

I came forth from the Father, and am come into the world: again, I leave the world, and go to the Father. *St. John* xvi. 19-28.

Disciples. We believe that Thou camest forth from God.

Do ye now believe? Behold, the hour cometh, yea, is now come, that ye shall be scattered, every man to his own, and shall leave Me alone: and yet I am not alone, because the Father is with Me. These things I have spoken unto you, that in Me ye might have peace. In the world ye shall have tribulation: but be of good cheer; I have overcome the world. *St. John* xvi. 31-33.

The Great Intercession.

Father, the hour is come; glorify Thy Son, that Thy Son also may glorify Thee: as Thou hast given Him power over all flesh, that He should give eternal life to as many as Thou hast given Him.

And this is life eternal, that they might know Thee the only true God, and Jesus Christ, whom Thou hast sent. I have glorified Thee on the earth: I have finished the work which Thou gavest Me to do.

And now, O Father, glorify Thou Me with Thine own self with the glory which I had with Thee before the world was. I have manifested Thy Name unto the men which Thou gavest Me out of the world: Thine they were, and Thou gavest them Me; and they have kept Thy word. Now they have known that all things whatsoever Thou hast given Me are of Thee. For I have given unto them the words which Thou gavest Me; and they have received them, and have known surely that I came out from Thee, and they have believed that Thou didst send Me.

I pray for them: I pray not for the world, but for them which Thou hast given Me; for they are Thine. And all Mine are Thine, and Thine are Mine; and I am glorified in them. And now I am no more in the world, but these are in the world, and I come to Thee.

Holy Father, keep through Thine own Name those whom Thou hast given Me, that they may be one, as we are. While I was with them in the world, I kept them in Thy Name: those that Thou gavest Me I have kept, and none of them is lost, but the son of perdition; that the Scripture might be fulfilled. And now come I to Thee; and these things I speak in the world, that they might have My joy fulfilled in themselves. I have given them Thy word ; and the world hath hated them, because they are not of the world, even as I am not of the world.

I pray not that Thou shouldest take them out of the world, but that Thou shouldest keep them from the evil. They are not of the world, even as I am not of the world.

Sanctify them through Thy truth : Thy word is truth. As Thou hast sent Me into the world, even so have I also sent them into the world. And for their sakes I sanctify Myself, that they also might be sanctified through the truth.

Neither pray I for these alone, but for them also which shall believe on Me through their word ; that they all may be one ; as Thou, Father, art in Me, and I in Thee, that they also may be one in us : that the world may believe that Thou hast sent Me.

And the glory which Thou gavest Me I have given them ; that they may be one, even as we are one : I in them, and Thou in Me, that they may be made perfect in one ; and that the world may know that Thou hast sent Me, and hast loved them, as Thou hast loved Me.

Father, I will that they also, whom Thou hast given Me, be with Me where I am ; that they may behold My glory, which Thou hast given Me : for Thou lovedst Me before the foundation of the world.

O righteous Father, the world hath not known Thee : but I have known Thee, and these have known that Thou hast sent Me. And I have declared unto them Thy Name, and will declare it : that the love wherewith Thou hast loved Me may be in them, and I in them. *St. John* xvii.

Second Warning to Peter.
Mount of Olives.

All ye shall be offended because of Me this night: for it is written, I will smite the shepherd, and the sheep of the flock shall be scattered abroad.

But after I am risen again, I will go before you into Galilee.

Peter. *Though all should be offended because of Thee, yet will I never be offended.*

Verily I say unto thee, That this day, even in this night, before the cock crow twice, thou shalt deny Me thrice. *St. Matt.* xxvi. 31, 34.
(Cf. *St. Mark* xiv. 27–30.)

The Agony in Gethsemane.
To the Disciples.

Sit ye here, while I go and pray yonder.
St. Matt. xxvi. 36.

Pray that ye enter not into temptation.
St. Luke xxii. 40.
(Cf. *St. Mark* xiv. 32.)

To Peter and James and John.

My soul is exceeding sorrowful, even unto death: tarry ye here, and watch with Me.
St. Matt. xxvi. 38.
(Cf. *St. Mark* xiv. 34.)

(*He fell on His face.*)

Abba, Father, all things are possible unto Thee; take away this cup from Me: nevertheless not what I will, but what Thou wilt. *St. Mark* xiv. 36.
(Cf. *St. Matt.* xxvi. 39.)

To Peter, and to the Two Brothers.

Simon, sleepest thou? couldest not thou watch one hour? Watch ye and pray, lest ye enter into temptation. The spirit truly is ready, but the flesh is weak. *St. Mark* xiv. 37, 38.
(Cf. *St. Matt.* xxvi. 40, 41.)

(*He prayed twice, using the same words.*)

O My Father, if this cup may not pass away from Me, except I drink it, Thy will be done.
St. Matt. xxvi. 42.

To the Disciples, after the Third Prayer.

Sleep on now, and take your rest: behold, the hour is at hand, and the Son of man is betrayed into the hands of sinners. Rise, let us be going: behold, he is at hand that doth betray Me.
St. Matt. xxvi. 45, 46.
(Cf. *St. Mark* xiv. 41, 42.)

Our Lord betrayed and taken.

Judas. Hail, Master!

Friend, wherefore art thou come?[1] Judas, betrayest thou the Son of man with a kiss?[2]

[1] *St. Matt.* xxvi. 50; [2] *St. Luke* xxii. 48.

To the Band of Men and Officers.

Whom seek ye?

Officers. Jesus of Nazareth.

I am He.

(*They fell to the ground.*)

Whom seek ye?

Officers. Jesus of Nazareth.

I have told you that I am He: if therefore ye seek Me, let these go their way. *St. John* xviii. 4–8.

To Peter.

Put up again thy sword into his place: for all they that take the sword shall perish with the sword.

Thinkest thou that I cannot now pray to My Father, and He shall presently give Me more than twelve legions of angels? But how then shall the Scripture be fulfilled, that thus it must be?

St. Matt. xxvi. 52–54.

The cup which My Father hath given Me, shall I not drink it? *St. John* xviii. 11.

Suffer ye thus far. *St. Luke* xxii. 51.

To the Multitudes.

Are ye come out as against a thief with swords and staves for to take Me? I sat daily with you teaching in the temple, and ye laid no hold on Me.[1] But this is your hour, and the power of darkness.[2] The Scriptures must be fulfilled.[3]

[1] *St. Matt.* xxvi. 55 : [2] *St. Luke* xxii. 53 : [3] *St. Mark* xiv. 48.

In the High Priest's House.

To Caiaphas (*asking Him of His doctrine*).

I spake openly to the world; I ever taught in the synagogue, and in the temple, whither the Jews always resort; and in secret have I said nothing. Why askest thou Me? ask them which heard Me, what I have said unto them: behold, they know what I said.

An officer. *Answerest Thou the high priest so?*

If I have spoken evil, bear witness of the evil: but if well, why smitest thou Me?

St. John xviii. 20-23.

Caiaphas. *I adjure Thee by the living God, that Thou tell us whether Thou be the Christ, the Son of God.*

I am: and ye shall see the Son of man sitting on the right hand of power, and coming in the clouds of heaven. *St. Mark* xiv. 62.
(Cf. *St. Matt.* xxvi. 64.)

SIXTH DAY OF THE WEEK.
FEAST OF THE PASSOVER.
(GOOD FRIDAY.)

April 7.

CHIEF EVENTS.

JESUS BROUGHT BEFORE PILATE	*St. Luke* xxiii. 1–6.
SENT BY HIM TO HEROD	*St. Luke* xxiii. 7–11.
THE SCOURGING	*St. John* xix. 1.
JESUS CONDEMNED TO DEATH	*St. John* xix. 2–16.
THE WAY OF THE CROSS	*St. Luke* xxiii. 25–32.
THE CRUCIFIXION	*St. Luke* xxiii. 33–49.
THE BURIAL	*St. Luke* xxiii. 50–56.

Before the Chief Priests' and Scribes' Council.

As soon as it was Day.

The council. *Art Thou the Christ? tell us.*

If I tell you, ye will not believe: and if I also ask you, ye will not answer Me, nor let Me go. Hereafter shall the Son of man sit on the right hand of the power of God.   *St. Luke* xxii. 67-69.

The council. *Art Thou then the Son of God?*

Ye say that I am.   *St. Luke* xxii. 70.

Before Pilate.

The Hall of Judgment.

Pilate. *Art Thou the King of the Jews?*

Sayest thou this thing of thyself, or did others tell it thee of Me?

Pilate. *The chief priests have delivered Thee unto me. What hast Thou done?*

My kingdom is not of this world: if My kingdom were of this world, then would My servants fight, that I should not be delivered to the Jews: but now is My kingdom not from hence.

Pilate.   *Art Thou the King of the Jews?*

Thou sayest that I am a King.   To this end was I born, and for this cause came I into the world, that I should bear witness unto the truth.   Every one that is of the truth heareth My voice.

St. John xviii. 34–37.

(Cf. *St. Matt.* xxvii. 11 ; *St. Mark* xv. 2 ; *St. Luke* xxiii. 3.)

Ecce Homo!

In the Judgment-Hall the Last Time.

Pilate.   *Knowest Thou not that I have power to crucify Thee?*

Thou couldest have no power at all against Me, except it were given thee from above : therefore he that delivered Me unto thee hath the greater sin.

St. John xix. 11.

The Way of the Cross.

To the Women which bewailed Him.

Daughters of Jerusalem, weep not for Me, but weep for yourselves, and for your children.   For, behold, the days are coming, in the which they shall say, Blessed are the barren, and the wombs that never bare, and the paps which never gave suck.   Then shall they begin to say to the mountains, Fall on us ; and to the hills, Cover us.   For if they do these things in a green tree, what shall be done in the dry?

St. Luke xxiii. 28–31.

The Words upon the Cross.

Father, forgive them; for they know not what they do. *St. Luke* xxiii. 34.

Verily I say unto thee, To-day shalt thou be with Me in Paradise. *St. Luke* xxiii. 42.

Woman, behold thy Son!
Behold thy Mother! *St. John* xix. 26, 27.

Eloi, Eloi, lama sabachthani? *St. Mark* xv. 34.
(Cf. *St. Matt.* xxvii. 46.)

I thirst. *St. John* xix. 28.

It is finished. *St. John* xix. 30.

Father, into Thy Hands I commend My Spirit. *St. Luke* xxiii. 46.

SIXTH PERIOD.

THE GREAT FORTY DAYS.

FIRST DAY OF THE WEEK.

(EASTER DAY.)

April 9, A.D. 29.

THE APPEARANCES RECORDED OF OUR LORD AFTER HIS RESURRECTION.

ON EASTER DAY.

1. To Mary Magdalene, at the Sepulchre, near Calvary . . . . *St. John* xx. 11-18.
2. To the Women, on their Way from the Sepulchre
St. Matt. xxviii. 9, 10.
3. To St. Peter . . . . . 1 *Cor.* xv. 5; *St. Luke* xxiv. 34.
4. To Cleopas and Another Disciple, on the Way to Emmaus . . . . *St. Luke* xxiv. 13-31.
5. To Ten of the Apostles at Evening, in the Chamber with closed Doors at Jerusalem . . *St. John* xx. 19-23.

EIGHT DAYS LATER.
(Low Sunday.)

6. To the Ten again, and St. Thomas . *St. John* xx. 26-29.

---

7. To Seven Apostles, by the Sea of Tiberias, in Galilee . . . . *St. John* xxi. 1-22 (cf. *St. Matt.* xxviii. 10).
8. To the Eleven, on a Mountain in Galilee
St. Matt. xxviii. 16-20.
9. To Five Hundred Brethren: Galilee . . 1 *Cor.* xv. 6.
10. To St. James: Jerusalem . . . . 1 *Cor.* xv. 7.
11. To the Apostles whom He had chosen: Jerusalem . . . . *Acts* i. 4-8.
12. To the Witnesses of the Ascension: on the Way from Jerusalem to Bethany *St. Luke* xxiv. l50, 51; *Acts* i. 9.

The First Appearance.

AT THE SEPULCHRE: EASTER MORNING.

To Mary Magdalene.

Woman, why weepest thou? whom seekest thou?

Mary Magdalene. If Thou hast borne Him hence, tell me where Thou hast laid Him.

Mary!

Mary Magdalene. Rabboni!

Touch Me not; for I am not yet ascended to My Father: but go to My brethren, and say unto them, I ascend unto My Father, and your Father; and to My God, and your God. *St. John* xx. 15-17.

The Second Appearance.

To the Women, on their Way from the Sepulchre.

All hail! Be not afraid: go tell My brethren that they go into Galilee, and there shall they see Me. *St. Matt.* xxviii. 9, 10.

The Fourth Appearance.

ON THE WAY TO EMMAUS: EASTER EVENING.

To Cleopas and Another Disciple.

What manner of communications are these that ye have one to another, as ye walk, and are sad?

Cleopas. *Art Thou only a stranger in Jerusalem, and hast not known the things which are come to pass?*

What things? *St. Luke* xxiv. 17–19.

Disciples. *Concerning Jesus of Nazareth. . . . We trusted that it had been He which should have redeemed Israel.*

O fools, and slow of heart to believe all that the prophets have spoken: ought not Christ to have suffered these things, and to enter into His glory? *St. Luke* xxiv. 25, 26.

The Fifth Appearance: The Commission to the Apostles.

JERUSALEM: EASTER EVENING.

To the Apostles.

Peace be unto you!

(*They were terrified.*)

Why are ye troubled? and why do thoughts arise in your hearts? Behold My hands and My feet, that it is I myself: handle Me, and see; for a spirit hath not flesh and bones, as ye see Me have. *St. Luke* xxiv. 36–39.
(Cf. *St. John* xx. 19.)

(*He shewed them His hands and His feet.*)

Peace be unto you: as My Father hath sent Me, even so send I you. *St. John* xx. 21.

(*He breathed on them.*)

Receive ye the Holy Ghost: whose soever sins ye remit, they are remitted unto them; and whose soever sins ye retain, they are retained.
St. John xx. 22, 23.

Have ye here any meat? *St. Luke* xxiv. 41.

(*He did eat before them.*)

These are the words which I spake unto you, while I was yet with you, that all things must be fulfilled, which were written in the Law of Moses, and in the prophets, and in the psalms, concerning Me.

Thus it is written, and thus it behoved Christ to suffer, and to rise from the dead the third day: and that repentance and remission of sins should be preached in His Name among all nations, beginning at Jerusalem. And ye are witnesses of these things. *St. Luke* xxiv. 44, 46-48.

The Sixth Appearance.

JERUSALEM: WHEN THE DOORS WERE SHUT, EIGHT DAYS AFTER THE RESURRECTION.

(LOW SUNDAY EVENING.)

To the Eleven Disciples.

Peace be unto you.

To Thomas.

Reach hither thy finger, and behold My hands; and reach hither thy hand, and thrust it into My side: and be not faithless, but believing.

Thomas. *My Lord and my God.*

Thomas, because thou hast seen Me, thou hast believed: blessed are they that have not seen, and yet have believed. *St. John* xx. 26-29.

The Seventh Appearance.

AT THE SEA OF TIBERIAS.

To Peter, Thomas, Nathanael, James, and John, and Two other Disciples.

Children, have ye any meat?

Disciples. No.

Cast the net on the right side of the ship, and ye shall find.

Bring of the fish which ye have now caught.

Come and dine.

To Peter.

Simon, son of Jonas, lovest thou Me more than these?

Peter. Yea, Lord; Thou knowest that I love Thee.

Feed My lambs.

Simon, son of Jonas, lovest thou Me?

Peter. Yea, Lord; Thou knowest that I love Thee.

Feed My sheep.

Simon, son of Jonas, lovest thou Me?

Peter. Lord, . . . Thou knowest that I love Thee.

Feed My sheep.

Verily, verily, I say unto thee, When thou wast young, thou girdedst thyself, and walkedst whither thou wouldest: but when thou shalt be old, thou shalt stretch forth thy hands and another shall gird thee, and carry thee whither thou wouldest not.

Follow Me.

Peter, seeing St. John. Lord, and what shall this man do?

If I will that he tarry till I come, what is that to thee? follow thou Me.   *St. John* xxi. 5–22.

The Eighth Appearance.

THE MOUNTAIN IN GALILEE.

To the Eleven Disciples.

All power is given unto Me in heaven and in earth. Go ye therefore, and teach all nations, baptizing them in the Name of the Father, and of the Son, and of the Holy Ghost: teaching them to observe all things whatsoever I have commanded you: and lo, I am with you alway, even unto the end of the world. Amen. *St. Matt.* xxviii. 18–20.

He that believeth and is baptized shall be saved; but he that believeth not shall be damned. And these signs shall follow them that believe; In My Name shall they cast out devils; they shall speak with new tongues; they shall take up serpents; and if they drink any deadly thing, it shall not hurt them; they shall lay hands on the sick, and they shall recover. *St. Mark* xvi. 16–18.

The Eleventh Appearance.

JERUSALEM: BEFORE THE ASCENSION.

To the Apostles.

And, behold, I send the promise of My Father upon you: but tarry ye in the city of Jerusalem, until ye be endued with power from on high.

St. Luke xxiv. 49.

Wait for the promise of the Father, which ye have heard of Me. For John truly baptized with water; but ye shall be baptized with the Holy Ghost not many days hence. *Acts* i. 4, 5.

Disciples. Lord, wilt Thou at this time restore again the kingdom to Israel?

It is not for you to know the times or the seasons, which the Father hath put in His own power. But ye shall receive power, after that the Holy Ghost is come upon you: and ye shall be witnesses unto Me both in Jerusalem, and in all Judæa, and in Samaria, and unto the uttermost part of the earth. *Acts* i. 7, 8.

Remember the words of the Lord Jesus, how He said,
It is more blessed to give than to receive.

Acts xx. 35.

# THE WORDS OF OUR INCARNATE LORD JESUS CHRIST, FROM HEAVEN, RECORDED IN THE ACTS OF THE APOSTLES.

Conversion of St. Paul.

ON THE ROAD FROM JERUSALEM TO DAMASCUS.
A.D. 35.

Saul, Saul, why persecutest thou Me? it is hard for thee to kick against the pricks. *Acts* xxvi. 14.

Saul. *Who art Thou, Lord?*

I am Jesus of Nazareth, Whom thou persecutest. *Acts* xxii. 8.

But rise, and stand upon thy feet: for I have appeared unto thee for this purpose, to make thee a minister and a witness both of these things which thou hast seen, and of those things in the which I will appear unto thee: delivering thee from the people, and from the Gentiles, unto whom now I send thee, to open their eyes, and to turn them from darkness to light, and from the power of Satan unto God, that they may receive forgiveness of sins, and inheritance among them which are sanctified by faith that is in Me. *Acts* xxvi. 16–18.

Saul. *What shall I do, Lord?*

Arise, and go into Damascus; and there it shall be told thee of all things which are appointed for thee to do. *Acts* xxii. 10.

The Commission to Ananias.

DAMASCUS.

Ananias.

Ananias. Behold, I am here, Lord.

Arise, and go into the street which is called Straight, and inquire in the house of Judas for one called Saul, of Tarsus: for, behold, he prayeth, and hath seen in a vision a man named Ananias coming in, and putting *his* hand on him, that he might receive his sight.

Ananias. Lord, *I have heard by many of this man, etc.*

Go thy way: for he is a chosen vessel unto Me, to bear My Name before the Gentiles, and kings, and the children of Israel: for I will show him how great things he must suffer for My Name's sake. *Acts* ix. 10–16.

To St. Paul, in the Temple.
JERUSALEM.

Make haste, and get thee quickly out of Jerusalem: for they will not receive thy testimony concerning Me.

St. Paul. Lord, they know how I imprisoned and beat in every synagogue them that believed on Thee.

Depart: for I will send thee far hence unto the Gentiles. *Acts* xxii. 18–21.

To St. Paul, when taken Prisoner.
THE CASTLE AT JERUSALEM.
A.D. 60 (?).

Be of good cheer, Paul: for as thou hast testified of Me in Jerusalem, so must thou bear witness also at Rome. *Acts* xxiii. 11.

A Selection of Works
IN
THEOLOGICAL LITERATURE
PUBLISHED BY
Messrs. LONGMANS, GREEN, & CO.
39 Paternoster Row, London, E.C.

Abbey and Overton.—THE ENGLISH CHURCH IN THE EIGHTEENTH CENTURY. By Charles J. Abbey, M.A., Rector of Checkendon, Reading, and John H. Overton, M.A., Rector of Epworth; Rural Dean of Isle of Axholme. *Crown 8vo.* 7s. 6d.

Adams.—SACRED ALLEGORIES. The Shadow of the Cross—The Distant Hills—The Old Man's Home—The King's Messengers. By the Rev. William Adams, M.A. *Crown 8vo.* 3s. 6d.

The four Allegories may be had separately, with Illustrations. 16mo. 1s. each.

Aids to the Inner Life.
Edited by the Rev. W. H. Hutchings, M.A., Rector of Kirkby Misperton, Yorkshire. *Five Vols.* 32mo, *cloth limp*, 6d. *each; or cloth extra*, 1s. *each.*

With red borders, 2s. *each. Sold separately.*

OF THE IMITATION OF CHRIST. By Thomas à Kempis.
THE CHRISTIAN YEAR.
THE DEVOUT LIFE. By St. Francis de Sales.
THE HIDDEN LIFE OF THE SOUL.
THE SPIRITUAL COMBAT. By Laurence Scupoli.

Allen.—THE CHURCH CATECHISM: its History and Contents. A Manual for Teachers and Students. By the Rev. A. J. C. Allen, M.A., formerly Principal of the Chester Diocesan Training College. *Crown 8vo.* 3s. 6d.

Barnes.—CANONICAL AND UNCANONICAL GOSPELS. With a Translation of the recently discovered Fragment of the 'Gospel of St. Peter,' and a Selection from the Sayings of our Lord not recorded in the Four Gospels. By W. E. Barnes, B.D., Theological Lecturer at Clare College, Cambridge. *Crown 8vo.* 3s. 6d.

Barry.—SOME LIGHTS OF SCIENCE ON THE FAITH. Being the Bampton Lectures for 1892. By the Right Rev. Alfred Barry, D.D., Canon of Windsor, formerly Bishop of Sydney, Metropolitan of New South Wales, and Primate of Australia. *8vo.* 12s. 6d.

Bathe.—Works by the Rev. ANTHONY BATHE, M.A.
  A LENT WITH JESUS. A Plain Guide for Churchmen. Containing Readings for Lent and Easter Week, and on the Holy Eucharist. 32mo, 1s.; or in paper cover, 6d.
  AN ADVENT WITH JESUS. 32mo, 1s.; or in paper cover, 6d.
  WHAT I SHOULD BELIEVE. A Simple Manual of Self-Instruction for Church People. Crown 8vo. 3s. 6d.

Benson.—THE FINAL PASSOVER: A Series of Meditations upon the Passion of our Lord Jesus Christ. By the Rev. R. M. BENSON, M.A., Student of Christ Church, Oxford. Small 8vo.
  Vol. I.—THE REJECTION. 5s.   Vol. III.—THE DIVINE EXODUS.
  Vol. II.—THE UPPER CHAMBER.   Parts I. and II. 5s. each.
  [In preparation.
  Vol. IV.—THE LIFE BEYOND THE GRAVE. 5s.

Bickersteth.—YESTERDAY, TO-DAY, AND FOR EVER: a Poem in Twelve Books. By EDWARD HENRY BICKERSTETH, D.D., Bishop of Exeter. One Shilling Edition, 18mo. With red borders, 16mo, 2s. 6d.
  The Crown 8vo Edition (5s.) may still be had.

Blunt.—Works by the Rev. JOHN HENRY BLUNT, D.D.
  THE ANNOTATED BOOK OF COMMON PRAYER: Being an Historical, Ritual, and Theological Commentary on the Devotional System of the Church of England. 4to. 21s.
  THE COMPENDIOUS EDITION OF THE ANNOTATED BOOK OF COMMON PRAYER: Forming a concise Commentary on the Devotional System of the Church of England. Crown 8vo. 10s. 6d.
  DICTIONARY OF DOCTRINAL AND HISTORICAL THEOLOGY. By various Writers. Imperial 8vo. 21s.
  DICTIONARY OF SECTS, HERESIES, ECCLESIASTICAL PARTIES AND SCHOOLS OF RELIGIOUS THOUGHT. By various Writers. Imperial 8vo. 21s.
  THE BOOK OF CHURCH LAW. Being an Exposition of the Legal Rights and Duties of the Parochial Clergy and the Laity of the Church of England. Revised by Sir WALTER G. F. PHILLIMORE, Bart., D.C.L. Crown 8vo. 7s. 6d.
  A COMPANION TO THE BIBLE: Being a Plain Commentary on Scripture History, to the end of the Apostolic Age. Two Vols. small 8vo. Sold separately.
    THE OLD TESTAMENT. 3s. 6d.   THE NEW TESTAMENT. 3s. 6d.
  HOUSEHOLD THEOLOGY: a Handbook of Religious Information respecting the Holy Bible, the Prayer Book, the Church, etc., etc. Paper cover, 16mo. 1s. Also the Larger Edition, 3s. 6d.

Body.—Works by the Rev. GEORGE BODY, D.D., Canon of Durham.
  THE LIFE OF LOVE. A Course of Lent Lectures. Crown 8vo. 4s. 6d.
  THE SCHOOL OF CALVARY; or, Laws of Christian Life revealed from the Cross. 16mo. 2s. 6d.
  THE LIFE OF JUSTIFICATION. 16mo. 2s. 6d.
  THE LIFE OF TEMPTATION. 16mo. 2s. 6d.

Bonney.—CHRISTIAN DOCTRINES AND MODERN THOUGHT: being the Boyle Lectures for 1891. By the Rev. T. G. BONNEY, D.Sc., Hon. Canon of Manchester. *Crown 8vo.* 5s.

Boultbee.—A COMMENTARY ON THE THIRTY-NINE ARTICLES OF THE CHURCH OF ENGLAND. By the Rev. T. P. BOULTBEE, formerly Principal of the London College of Divinity, St. John's Hall, Highbury. *Crown 8vo.* 6s.

Bright.—Works by WILLIAM BRIGHT, D.D., Canon of Christ Church, Oxford.
WAYMARKS IN CHURCH HISTORY. *Crown 8vo.*
MORALITY IN DOCTRINE. *Crown 8vo.* 7s. 6d.
LESSONS FROM THE LIVES OF THREE GREAT FATHERS: St. Athanasius, St. Chrysostom, and St. Augustine. *Crown 8vo.* 6s.
THE INCARNATION AS A MOTIVE POWER. *Crown 8vo.* 6s.

Bright and Medd.—LIBER PRECUM PUBLICARUM ECCLESIÆ ANGLICANÆ. A GULIELMO BRIGHT, S.T.P., et PETRO GOLDSMITH MEDD, A.M., Latine redditus. *Small 8vo.* 7s. 6d.

Browne.—AN EXPOSITION OF THE THIRTY-NINE ARTICLES, Historical and Doctrinal. By E. H. BROWNE, D.D., formerly Bishop of Winchester. *8vo.* 16s.

Campion and Beamont.—THE PRAYER BOOK INTERLEAVED. With Historical Illustrations and Explanatory Notes arranged parallel to the Text. By W. M. CAMPION, D.D., and W. J. BEAMONT, M.A. *Small 8vo.* 7s. 6d.

Carter.—Works edited by the Rev. T. T. CARTER, M.A., Hon. Canon of Christ Church, Oxford.
THE TREASURY OF DEVOTION: a Manual of Prayer for General and Daily Use. Compiled by a Priest. 18mo. 2s. 6d.; *cloth limp,* 2s.; *or bound with the Book of Common Prayer,* 3s. 6d. *Large-Type Edition. Crown 8vo.* 3s. 6d.
THE WAY OF LIFE: A Book of Prayers and Instruction for the Young at School, with a Preparation for Confirmation. Compiled by a Priest, 18mo. 1s. 6d.
THE PATH OF HOLINESS: a First Book of Prayers, with the Service of the Holy Communion, for the Young. Compiled by a Priest. With Illustrations. 16mo. 1s. 6d.; *cloth limp,* 1s.
THE GUIDE TO HEAVEN: a Book of Prayers for every Want. (For the Working Classes.) Compiled by a Priest. 18mo. 1s. 6d.; *cloth limp,* 1s. *Large-Type Edition. Crown 8vo.* 1s. 6d.; *cloth limp,* 1s.

[continued.

Carter.—Works edited by the Rev. T. T. CARTER, M.A., Hon. Canon of Christ Church, Oxford—*continued.*
SELF-RENUNCIATION. 16mo. 2s. 6d.
THE STAR OF CHILDHOOD: a First Book of Prayers and Instruction for Children. Compiled by a Priest. With Illustrations. 16mo. 2s. 6d.
NICHOLAS FERRAR: his Household and his Friends. With Portrait engraved after a Picture by CORNELIUS JANSSEN at Magdalene College, Cambridge. *Crown 8vo. 6s.*

Carter.—MAXIMS AND GLEANINGS FROM THE WRITINGS OF T. T. CARTER, M.A. Selected and arranged for Daily Use. *Crown 16mo. 1s.*

Conybeare and Howson.—THE LIFE AND EPISTLES OF ST. PAUL. By the Rev. W. J. CONYBEARE, M.A., and the Very Rev. J. S. HOWSON, D.D. With numerous Maps and Illustrations.
LIBRARY EDITION. *Two Vols. 8vo. 21s.*
STUDENTS' EDITION. *One Vol. Crown 8vo. 6s.*
POPULAR EDITION. *One Vol. Crown 8vo. 3s. 6d.*

Copleston.—BUDDHISM—PRIMITIVE AND PRESENT IN MAGADHA AND IN CEYLON. By REGINALD STEPHEN COPLESTON, D.D., Bishop of Colombo. 8vo. 16s.

Devotional Series, 16mo, Red Borders. *Each 2s. 6d.*
BICKERSTETH'S YESTERDAY, TO-DAY, AND FOR EVER.
CHILCOT'S TREATISE ON EVIL THOUGHTS.
THE CHRISTIAN YEAR.
FRANCIS DE SALES' (ST.) THE DEVOUT LIFE.
HERBERT'S POEMS AND PROVERBS.
KEMPIS' (À) OF THE IMITATION OF CHRIST.
WILSON'S THE LORD'S SUPPER. *Large type.*
*TAYLOR'S (JEREMY) HOLY LIVING.
*——   ——   HOLY DYING.
  * *These two in one Volume.* 5s.

Devotional Series, 18mo, without Red Borders. *Each 1s.*
BICKERSTETH'S YESTERDAY, TO-DAY, AND FOR EVER.
THE CHRISTIAN YEAR.
FRANCIS DE SALES' (ST.) THE DEVOUT LIFE.
HERBERT'S POEMS AND PROVERBS.
KEMPIS (À) OF THE IMITATION OF CHRIST.
WILSON'S THE LORD'S SUPPER, *Large type.*
*TAYLOR'S (JEREMY) HOLY LIVING.
*——   ——   HOLY DYING.
  * *These two in one Volume.* 2s. 6d.

IN THEOLOGICAL LITERATURE.

Edersheim.—Works by ALFRED EDERSHEIM, M.A., D.D., Ph.D., sometime Grinfield Lecturer on the Septuagint, Oxford.

THE LIFE AND TIMES OF JESUS THE MESSIAH. *Two Vols.* 8vo. 24s.

JESUS THE MESSIAH: being an Abridged Edition of 'The Life and Times of Jesus the Messiah.' *Crown 8vo.* 7s. 6d.

PROPHECY AND HISTORY IN RELATION TO THE MESSIAH: The Warburton Lectures, 1880-1884. 8vo. 12s.

Ellicott.—Works by C. J. ELLICOTT, D.D., Bishop of Gloucester and Bristol.

A CRITICAL AND GRAMMATICAL COMMENTARY ON ST. PAUL'S EPISTLES. Greek Text, with a Critical and Grammatical Commentary, and a Revised English Translation. 8vo.

1 CORINTHIANS. 16s.
GALATIANS. 8s. 6d.
EPHESIANS. 8s. 6d.

PHILIPPIANS, COLOSSIANS, AND PHILEMON. 10s. 6d.
THESSALONIANS. 7s. 6d.

PASTORAL EPISTLES. 10s. 6d.

HISTORICAL LECTURES ON THE LIFE OF OUR LORD JESUS CHRIST. 8vo. 12s.

Epochs of Church History.—Edited by MANDELL CREIGHTON, D.D., LL.D., Bishop of Peterborough. *Fcap. 8vo. 2s. 6d. each.*

THE ENGLISH CHURCH IN OTHER LANDS. By the Rev. H. W. TUCKER, M.A.

THE HISTORY OF THE REFORMATION IN ENGLAND. By the Rev. GEO. G. PERRY, M.A.

THE CHURCH OF THE EARLY FATHERS. By the Rev. ALFRED PLUMMER, D.D.

THE EVANGELICAL REVIVAL IN THE EIGHTEENTH CENTURY. By the Rev. J. H. OVERTON, M.A.

THE UNIVERSITY OF OXFORD. By the Hon. G. C. BRODRICK, D.C.L.

THE UNIVERSITY OF CAMBRIDGE. By J. BASS MULLINGER, M.A.

THE ENGLISH CHURCH IN THE MIDDLE AGES. By the Rev. W. HUNT, M.A.

THE CHURCH AND THE EASTERN EMPIRE. By the Rev. H. F. TOZER, M.A.

THE CHURCH AND THE ROMAN EMPIRE. By the Rev. A. CARR.

THE CHURCH AND THE PURITANS, 1570-1660. By HENRY OFFLEY WAKEMAN, M.A.

HILDEBRAND AND HIS TIMES. By the Rev. W. R. W. STEPHENS, M.A.

THE POPES AND THE HOHENSTAUFEN. By UGO BALZANI.

THE COUNTER REFORMATION. By ADOLPHUS WILLIAM WARD, Litt. D.

WYCLIFFE AND MOVEMENTS FOR REFORM. By REGINALD L. POOLE, M.A.

THE ARIAN CONTROVERSY. By H. M. GWATKIN, M.A.

Fosbery.—Works edited by the Rev. THOMAS VINCENT FOSBERY, M.A., sometime Vicar of St. Giles's, Reading.

    VOICES OF COMFORT. *Cheap Edition. Small 8vo.* 3s. 6d.
        The Larger Edition (7s. 6d.) may still be had.

    HYMNS AND POEMS FOR THE SICK AND SUFFERING. In connection with the Service for the Visitation of the Sick. Selected from Various Authors. *Small 8vo.* 3s. 6d.

Gore.—Works by the Rev. CHARLES GORE, M.A., Principal of the Pusey House; Fellow of Trinity College, Oxford.

    THE MINISTRY OF THE CHRISTIAN CHURCH. 8vo. 10s. 6d.
    ROMAN CATHOLIC CLAIMS. *Crown 8vo.* 3s. 6d.

Goulburn.—Works by EDWARD MEYRICK GOULBURN, D.D., D.C.L., sometime Dean of Norwich.

    THOUGHTS ON PERSONAL RELIGION. *Small 8vo.* 6s. 6d. *Cheap Edition*, 3s. 6d.; *Presentation Edition*, 2 vols. small 8vo, 10s. 6d.

    THE PURSUIT OF HOLINESS: a Sequel to 'Thoughts on Personal Religion.' *Small 8vo.* 5s. *Cheap Edition.* 3s. 6d.

    THE GOSPEL OF THE CHILDHOOD: a Practical and Devotional Commentary on the Single Incident of our Blessed Lord's Childhood (St. Luke ii. 41 to the end). *Crown 8vo.* 2s. 6d.

    THE COLLECTS OF THE DAY: an Exposition, Critical and Devotional, of the Collects appointed at the Communion. With Preliminary Essays on their Structure, Sources, etc. 2 vols. *Crown 8vo.* 8s. each.

    THOUGHTS UPON THE LITURGICAL GOSPELS for the Sundays, one for each day in the year. With an Introduction on their Origin, History, the modifications made in them by the Reformers and by the Revisers of the Prayer Book. 2 vols. *Crown 8vo.* 16s.

    MEDITATIONS UPON THE LITURGICAL GOSPELS for the Minor Festivals of Christ, the two first Week-days of the Easter and Whitsun Festivals, and the Red-letter Saints' Days. *Crown 8vo.* 8s. 6d.

    FAMILY PRAYERS, compiled from various sources (chiefly from Bishop Hamilton's Manual), and arranged on the Liturgical Principle. *Crown 8vo.* 3s. 6d. *Cheap Edition*, 16mo. 1s.

Harrison.—Works by the Rev. ALEXANDER J. HARRISON, B.D., Lecturer of the Christian Evidence Society.

    PROBLEMS OF CHRISTIANITY AND SCEPTICISM; Lessons from Twenty Years' Experience in the Field of Christian Evidence. *Crown 8vo.* 7s. 6d.

    THE CHURCH IN RELATION TO SCEPTICS: a Conversational Guide to Evidential Work. *Crown 8vo.* 7s. 6d.

Holland.—Works by the Rev. HENRY SCOTT HOLLAND, M.A., Canon and Precentor of St. Paul's.

> THE CITY OF GOD AND THE COMING OF THE KINGDOM: Four Addresses delivered at St. Asaph on the Spiritual and Ethical Value of Belief in the Church. To which are added Sermons on kindred subjects. *Crown 8vo. 7s. 6d.*
>
> PLEAS AND CLAIMS FOR CHRIST. *Crown 8vo. 7s. 6d.*
>
> CREED AND CHARACTER: Sermons. *Crown 8vo. 3s. 6d.*
>
> ON BEHALF OF BELIEF. Sermons preached in St. Paul's Cathedral. *Crown 8vo. 3s. 6d.*
>
> CHRIST OR ECCLESIASTES. Sermons preached in St. Paul's Cathedral. *Crown 8vo. 2s. 6d.*
>
> LOGIC AND LIFE, with other Sermons. *Crown 8vo. 3s. 6d.*

Hopkins.—CHRIST THE CONSOLER. A Book of Comfort for the Sick. By ELLICE HOPKINS. *Small 8vo. 2s. 6d.*

Ingram.—HAPPINESS IN THE SPIRITUAL LIFE; or, 'The Secret of the Lord.' A Series of Practical Considerations. By W. CLAVELL INGRAM, D.D., Dean of Peterborough. *Crown 8vo. 7s. 6d.*

INHERITANCE OF THE SAINTS; or, Thoughts on the Communion of Saints and the Life of the World to come. Collected chiefly from English Writers by L. P. With a Preface by the Rev. HENRY SCOTT HOLLAND, M.A. *Crown 8vo. 7s. 6d.*

Jameson.—Works by Mrs. JAMESON.

> SACRED AND LEGENDARY ART, containing Legends of the Angels and Archangels, the Evangelists, the Apostles. With 19 Etchings and 187 Woodcuts. *Two vols. Cloth, gilt top, 20s. net.*
>
> LEGENDS OF THE MONASTIC ORDERS, as represented in the Fine Arts. With 11 Etchings and 88 Woodcuts. *One Vol. Cloth, gilt top, 10s. net.*
>
> LEGENDS OF THE MADONNA, OR BLESSED VIRGIN MARY. With 27 Etchings and 165 Woodcuts. *One Vol. Cloth, gilt top, 10s. net.*
>
> THE HISTORY OF OUR LORD, as exemplified in Works of Art. Commenced by the late Mrs. JAMESON; continued and completed by LADY EASTLAKE. With 31 Etchings and 281 Woodcuts. *Two Vols. 8vo. 20s. net.*

Jennings.—ECCLESIA ANGLICANA. A History of the Church of Christ in England from the Earliest to the Present Times. By the Rev. ARTHUR CHARLES JENNINGS, M.A. *Crown 8vo. 7s. 6d.*

Jukes.—Works by ANDREW JUKES.

THE NEW MAN AND THE ETERNAL LIFE. Notes on the Reiterated Amens of the Son of God. *Crown 8vo.* 6s.

THE NAMES OF GOD IN HOLY SCRIPTURE: a Revelation of His Nature and Relationships. *Crown 8vo.* 4s. 6d.

THE TYPES OF GENESIS. *Crown 8vo.* 7s. 6d.

THE SECOND DEATH AND THE RESTITUTION OF ALL THINGS. *Crown 8vo.* 3s. 6d.

THE MYSTERY OF THE KINGDOM. *Crown 8vo.* 2s. 6d.

THE ORDER AND CONNEXION OF THE CHURCH'S TEACHING, as set forth in the arrangement of the Epistles and Gospels throughout the Year. *Crown 8vo.* 2s. 6d.

King.—DR. LIDDON'S TOUR IN EGYPT AND PALESTINE IN 1886. Being Letters descriptive of the Tour, written by his Sister, Mrs. KING. *Crown 8vo.* 5s.

Knox Little.—Works by W. J. KNOX LITTLE, M.A., Canon Residentiary of Worcester, and Vicar of Hoar Cross.

SACERDOTALISM, WHEN RIGHTLY UNDERSTOOD, THE TEACHING OF THE CHURCH OF ENGLAND: being a Letter addressed in Four Parts to the Very Rev. WILLIAM J. BUTLER, D.D., Dean of Lincoln, etc., etc. *Crown 8vo.* 6s.; *or in Four Parts, price* 1s. *each net.*

    Part I. CONFESSION AND ABSOLUTION.
    Part II. FASTING COMMUNION AND EUCHARISTIC WORSHIP.
    Part III. THE REAL PRESENCE AND THE EUCHARISTIC SACRIFICE.
    Part IV. THE APOSTOLIC MINISTRY.

SKETCHES IN SUNSHINE AND STORM: a Collection of Miscellaneous Essays and Notes of Travel. *Crown 8vo.* 7s. 6d.

THE CHRISTIAN HOME. *Crown 8vo.* 6s. 6d.

THE HOPES AND DECISIONS OF THE PASSION OF OUR MOST HOLY REDEEMER. *Crown 8vo.* 2s. 6d.

CHARACTERISTICS AND MOTIVES OF THE CHRISTIAN LIFE. Ten Sermons preached in Manchester Cathedral, in Lent and Advent. *Crown 8vo.* 2s. 6d.

SERMONS PREACHED FOR THE MOST PART IN MANCHESTER. *Crown 8vo.* 3s. 6d.

THE MYSTERY OF THE PASSION OF OUR MOST HOLY REDEEMER. *Crown 8vo.* 2s. 6d.

[continued.

Knox Little.—Works by W. J. KNOX LITTLE, M.A., Canon Residentiary of Worcester, and Vicar of Hoar Cross.—*continued.*

THE WITNESS OF THE PASSION OF OUR MOST HOLY REDEEMER. *Crown 8vo.* 2s. 6d.

THE LIGHT OF LIFE. Sermons preached on Various Occasions. *Crown 8vo.* 3s. 6d.

SUNLIGHT AND SHADOW IN THE CHRISTIAN LIFE. Sermons preached for the most part in America. *Crown 8vo.* 3s. 6d.

Lear.—Works by, and Edited by, H. L. SIDNEY LEAR.

FOR DAYS AND YEARS. A book containing a Text, Short Reading, and Hymn for Every Day in the Church's Year. 16mo. 2s. 6d. *Also a Cheap Edition*, 32mo. 1s.; *or cloth gilt*, 1s. 6d.

FIVE MINUTES. Daily Readings of Poetry. 16mo. 3s. 6d. *Also a Cheap Edition*, 32mo. 1s.; *or cloth gilt*, 1s. 6d.

WEARINESS. A Book for the Languid and Lonely. *Large Type. Small 8vo.* 5s.

THE LIGHT OF THE CONSCIENCE. 16mo. 2s. 6d. 32mo. 1s.; *cloth limp*, 6d.

CHRISTIAN BIOGRAPHIES. *Nine Vols. Crown 8vo.* 3s. 6d. *each.*

- MADAME LOUISE DE FRANCE, Daughter of Louis XV., known also as the Mother Térèse de St. Augustin.
- A DOMINICAN ARTIST: a Sketch of the Life of the Rev. Père Besson, of the Order of St. Dominic.
- HENRI PERREYVE. By A. GRATRY.
- ST. FRANCIS DE SALES, Bishop and Prince of Geneva.
- THE REVIVAL OF PRIESTLY LIFE IN THE SEVENTEENTH CENTURY IN FRANCE.
- A CHRISTIAN PAINTER OF THE NINETEENTH CENTURY.
- BOSSUET AND HIS CONTEMPORARIES.
- FÉNELON, ARCHBISHOP OF CAMBRAI.
- HENRI DOMINIQUE LACORDAIRE.

DEVOTIONAL WORKS. Edited by H. L. SIDNEY LEAR. *New and Uniform Editions. Nine Vols.* 16mo. 2s. 6d. *each.*

- FÉNELON'S SPIRITUAL LETTERS TO MEN.
- FÉNELON'S SPIRITUAL LETTERS TO WOMEN.
- A SELECTION FROM THE SPIRITUAL LETTERS OF ST. FRANCIS DE SALES.
- THE SPIRIT OF ST. FRANCIS DE SALES.
- THE HIDDEN LIFE OF THE SOUL.
- THE LIGHT OF THE CONSCIENCE.
- SELF-RENUNCIATION. From the French.
- ST. FRANCIS DE SALES' OF THE LOVE OF GOD.
- SELECTIONS FROM PASCAL'S 'THOUGHTS.'

Liddon.—Works by HENRY PARRY LIDDON, D.D., D.C.L., LL.D., late Canon Residentiary and Chancellor of St. Paul's.

LIFE OF EDWARD BOUVERIE PUSEY, D.D. By HENRY PARRY LIDDON, D.D., D.C.L., LL.D. Edited and prepared for publication by the Rev. J. O. JOHNSTON, M.A., Vicar of All Saints', Oxford; and the Rev. ROBERT J. WILSON, M.A., Warden of Keble College. *Four Vols. 8vo. Vols. I. and II., with 2 Portraits and 7 Illustrations. 36s.*

ESSAYS AND ADDRESSES: Lectures on Buddhism—Lectures on the Life of St. Paul—Papers on Dante. *Crown 8vo. 5s.*

EXPLANATORY ANALYSIS OF PAUL'S EPISTLE TO THE ROMANS. 8vo. 14s.

SERMONS ON OLD TESTAMENT SUBJECTS. *Crown 8vo. 5s.*

SERMONS ON SOME WORDS OF CHRIST. *Crown 8vo. 5s.*

THE DIVINITY OF OUR LORD AND SAVIOUR JESUS CHRIST. Being the Bampton Lectures for 1866. *Crown 8vo. 5s.*

ADVENT IN ST. PAUL'S. Sermons bearing chiefly on the Two Comings of our Lord. *Two Vols. Crown 8vo. 3s. 6d. each. Cheap Edition in one Volume. Crown 8vo. 5s.*

CHRISTMASTIDE IN ST. PAUL'S. Sermons bearing chiefly on the Birth of our Lord and the End of the Year. *Crown 8vo. 5s.*

PASSIONTIDE SERMONS. *Crown 8vo. 5s.*

EASTER IN ST. PAUL'S. Sermons bearing chiefly on the Resurrection of our Lord. *Two Vols. Crown 8vo. 3s. 6d. each. Cheap Edition in one Volume. Crown 8vo. 5s.*

SERMONS PREACHED BEFORE THE UNIVERSITY OF OXFORD. *Two Vols. Crown 8vo. 3s. 6d. each. Cheap Edition in one Volume. Crown 8vo. 5s.*

THE MAGNIFICAT. Sermons in St. Paul's. *Crown 8vo. 2s. 6d.*

SOME ELEMENTS OF RELIGION. Lent Lectures. *Small 8vo. 2s. 6d.*; or in paper cover, 1s. 6d.
The Crown 8vo Edition (5s.) may still be had.

SELECTIONS FROM THE WRITINGS OF H. P. LIDDON, D.D. *Crown 8vo. 3s. 6d.*

MAXIMS AND GLEANINGS FROM THE WRITINGS OF H. P. LIDDON, D.D. Selected and arranged by C. M. S. *Crown 16mo. 1s.*

DR. LIDDON'S TOUR IN EGYPT AND PALESTINE IN 1886. Being Letters descriptive of the Tour, written by his Sister, Mrs. KING. *Crown 8vo. 5s.*

Luckock.—Works by HERBERT MORTIMER LUCKOCK, D.D., Dean of Lichfield.

> AFTER DEATH. An Examination of the Testimony of Primitive Times respecting the State of the Faithful Dead, and their Relationship to the Living. *Crown 8vo.* 6s.
>
> THE INTERMEDIATE STATE BETWEEN DEATH AND JUDGMENT. Being a Sequel to *After death*. *Crown 8vo.* 6s.
>
> FOOTPRINTS OF THE SON OF MAN, as traced by St. Mark. Being Eighty Portions for Private Study, Family Reading, and Instructions in Church. *Two Vols. Crown 8vo.* 12s. *Cheap Edition in one Vol. Crown 8vo.* 5s.
>
> THE DIVINE LITURGY. Being the Order for Holy Communion, Historically, Doctrinally, and devotionally set forth, in Fifty Portions. *Crown 8vo.* 6s.
>
> STUDIES IN THE HISTORY OF THE BOOK OF COMMON PRAYER. The Anglican Reform—The Puritan Innovations—The Elizabethan Reaction—The Caroline Settlement. With Appendices. *Crown 8vo.* 6s.
>
> THE BISHOPS IN THE TOWER. A Record of Stirring Events affecting the Church and Nonconformists from the Restoration to the Revolution. *Crown 8vo.* 6s.

LYRA GERMANICA. Hymns translated from the German by CATHERINE WINKWORTH. *Small 8vo.* 5s.

MacColl.—CHRISTIANITY IN RELATION TO SCIENCE AND MORALS. By the Rev. MALCOLM MACCOLL, M.A., Canon Residentiary of Ripon. *Crown 8vo.* 6s.

Mason.—Works by A. J. MASON, D.D., Hon. Canon of Canterbury and Examining Chaplain to the Archbishop of Canterbury.

> THE FAITH OF THE GOSPEL. A Manual of Christian Doctrine. *Crown 8vo.* 3s. 6d.
>
> THE RELATION OF CONFIRMATION TO BAPTISM. As taught in Holy Scripture and the Fathers. *Crown 8vo.* 7s. 6d.

Mercier.—OUR MOTHER CHURCH: Being Simple Talk on High Topics. By Mrs. JEROME MERCIER. *Small 8vo.* 3s. 6d.

Molesworth.—STORIES OF THE SAINTS FOR CHILDREN: The Black Letter Saints. By Mrs. MOLESWORTH, Author of 'The Palace in the Garden,' etc., etc. *With Illustrations. Royal 16mo.* 5s.

Mozley.—Works by J. B. MOZLEY, D.D., late Canon of Christ Church, and Regius Professor of Divinity at Oxford.

    ESSAYS, HISTORICAL AND THEOLOGICAL. *Two Vols. 8vo.* 24s.

    EIGHT LECTURES ON MIRACLES. Being the Bampton Lectures for 1865. *Crown 8vo.* 7s. 6d.

    RULING IDEAS IN EARLY AGES AND THEIR RELATION TO OLD TESTAMENT FAITH. Lectures delivered to Graduates of the University of Oxford. *8vo.* 10s. 6d.

    SERMONS PREACHED BEFORE THE UNIVERSITY OF OXFORD, and on Various Occasions. *Crown 8vo.* 7s. 6d.

    SERMONS, PAROCHIAL AND OCCASIONAL. *Crown 8vo.* 7s. 6d.

Newbolt.—Works by the Rev. W. C. E. NEWBOLT, M.A., Canon and Chancellor of St. Paul's Cathedral, Select Preacher at Oxford, and Examining Chaplain to the Lord Bishop of Ely.

    SPECULUM SACERDOTUM; or, the Divine Model of the Priestly Life. *Crown 8vo.* 7s. 6d.

    THE FRUIT OF THE SPIRIT. Being Ten Addresses bearing on the Spiritual Life. *Crown 8vo.* 2s. 6d.

    THE MAN OF GOD. Being Six Addresses delivered during Lent at the Primary Ordination of the Right Rev. the Lord Alwyne Compton, D.D., Bishop of Ely. *Small 8vo.* 1s. 6d.

    THE PRAYER BOOK: Its Voice and Teaching. Being Spiritual Addresses bearing on the Book of Common Prayer. *Crown 8vo.* 2s. 6d.

Newnham.—THE ALL-FATHER: Sermons preached in a Village Church. By the Rev. H. P. NEWNHAM. With Preface by EDNA LYALL. *Crown 8vo.* 4s. 6d.

Newman.—Works by JOHN HENRY NEWMAN, B.D., sometime Vicar of St. Mary's, Oxford.

PAROCHIAL AND PLAIN SERMONS. *Eight Vols. Cabinet Edition. Crown 8vo. 5s. each. Cheaper Edition. 3s. 6d. each.*

SELECTION, ADAPTED TO THE SEASONS OF THE ECCLESIASTICAL YEAR, from the 'Parochial and Plain Sermons,' *Cabinet Edition. Crown 8vo. 5s. Cheaper Edition. 3s. 6d.*

FIFTEEN SERMONS PREACHED BEFORE THE UNIVERSITY OF OXFORD *Cabinet Edition. Crown 8vo. 5s. Cheaper Edition. 3s. 6d.*

SERMONS BEARING UPON SUBJECTS OF THE DAY. *Cabinet Edition. Crown 8vo. 5s. Cheaper Edition. Crown 8vo. 3s. 6d.*

LECTURES ON THE DOCTRINE OF JUSTIFICATION. *Cabinet Edition Crown 8vo. 5s. Cheaper Edition. 3s. 6d.*

*** *A Complete List of Cardinal Newman's Works can be had on Application.*

Osborne.—Works by EDWARD OSBORNE, Mission Priest of the Society of St. John the Evangelist, Cowley, Oxford.

THE CHILDREN'S SAVIOUR. Instructions to Children on the Life of Our Lord and Saviour Jesus Christ. *Illustrated. 16mo. 2s. 6d.*

THE SAVIOUR KING. Instructions to Children on Old Testament Types and Illustrations of the Life of Christ. *Illustrated. 16mo. 2s. 6d.*

THE CHILDREN'S FAITH. Instructions to Children on the Apostles' Creed. *Illustrated. 16mo. 2s. 6d.*

Overton.—THE ENGLISH CHURCH IN THE NINETEENTH CENTURY. By the Rev. JOHN H. OVERTON, M.A., Canon of Lincoln, Rector of Epworth, Doncaster, and Rural Dean of the Isle of Axholme. *8vo. 14s.*

Oxenden.—Works by the Right Rev. ASHTON OXENDEN, formerly Bishop of Montreal.

PLAIN SERMONS, to which is prefixed a Memorial Portrait. *Crown 8vo. 5s.*

THE HISTORY OF MY LIFE: An Autobiography. *Crown 8vo. 5s.*

PEACE AND ITS HINDRANCES. *Crown 8vo. 1s. sewed, 2s. cloth.*

THE PATHWAY OF SAFETY; or, Counsel to the Awakened. *Fcap. 8vo, large type. 2s. 6d. Cheap Edition. Small type, limp, 1s.*

THE EARNEST COMMUNICANT. *New Red Rubric Edition. 32mo, cloth. 2s. Common Edition. 32mo. 1s.*

OUR CHURCH AND HER SERVICES. *Fcap. 8vo. 2s. 6d.*

[continued.

Oxenden.—Works by the Right Rev. ASHTON OXENDEN formerly Bishop of Montreal—*continued.*
FAMILY PRAYERS FOR FOUR WEEKS. First Series. *Fcap. 8vo.* 2s. 6d. Second Series. *Fcap. 8vo.* 2s. 6d.
    LARGE TYPE EDITION. Two Series in one Volume. *Crown 8vo.* 6s.
COTTAGE SERMONS; or, Plain Words to the Poor. *Fcap. 8vo.* 2s. 6d.
THOUGHTS FOR HOLY WEEK. 16mo, *cloth.* 1s. 6d.
DECISION. 18mo. 1s. 6d.
THE HOME BEYOND; or, A Happy Old Age. *Fcap. 8vo.* 1s. 6d.
THE LABOURING MAN'S BOOK. 18mo, *large type, cloth.* 1s. 6d.

Paget.—Works by FRANCIS PAGET, D.D., Dean of Christ Church, Oxford.
THE SPIRIT OF DISCIPLINE: Sermons. *Crown 8vo.* 6s. 6d.
FACULTIES AND DIFFICULTIES FOR BELIEF AND DISBELIEF. *Crown 8vo.* 6s. 6d.
THE HALLOWING OF WORK. Addresses given at Eton, January 16-18, 1888. *Small 8vo.* 2s.

PRACTICAL REFLECTIONS. By a CLERGYMAN. With Prefaces by H. P. LIDDON, D.D., D.C.L., and the BISHOP OF LINCOLN. *Crown 8vo.*
    THE HOLY GOSPELS. 4s. 6d. | THE PSALMS. 5s.
    ACTS TO REVELATIONS. 6s. | THE BOOK OF GENESIS. 4s. 6d.

PRIEST (THE) TO THE ALTAR; or, Aids to the Devout Celebration of Holy Communion, chiefly after the Ancient English Use of Sarum. *Royal 8vo.* 12s.

Puller.—THE PRIMITIVE SAINTS AND THE SEE OF ROME. By F. W. PULLER, M.A., Mission Priest of the Society of St. John Evangelist, Cowley, Oxford. *Crown 8vo.* 7s. 6d.

Pusey.—LIFE OF EDWARD BOUVERIE PUSEY, D.D. By HENRY PARRY LIDDON, D.D., D.C.L., LL.D. Edited and prepared for publication by the Rev. J. O. JOHNSTON, M.A., Vicar of All Saints', Oxford, and the Rev. ROBERT J. WILSON, M.A., Warden of Keble College. *Four Vols. 8vo. Vols. I. and II., with 2 Portraits and 7 Illustrations.* 36s.

Pusey.—Works by the Rev. E. B. PUSEY, D.D.
PRIVATE PRAYERS. With Preface by H. P. LIDDON, D.D. 32mo. 1s.
PRAYERS FOR A YOUNG SCHOOLBOY. With a Preface by H. P. LIDDON, D.D. 24mo. 1s.

Sanday.—Works by W. SANDAY, D.D., Dean Ireland's Professor of Exegesis and Fellow of Exeter College, Oxford.
  INSPIRATION: Eight Lectures on the Early History and Origin of the Doctrine of Biblical Inspiration. Being the Bampton Lectures for 1893. 8vo. 16s.
  THE ORACLES OF GOD: Nine Lectures on the Nature and Extent of Biblical Inspiration and the Special Significance of the Old Testament Scriptures at the Present Time. *Crown 8vo. 4s.*
  TWO PRESENT-DAY QUESTIONS. I. Biblical Criticism. II. The Social Movement. Sermons preached before the University of Cambridge. *Crown 8vo. 2s. 6d.*

Seebohm.—THE OXFORD REFORMERS—JOHN COLET, ERASMUS, AND THOMAS MORE: A History of their Fellow-Work. By FREDERICK SEEBOHM. 8vo. 14s.

Stanton.—THE PLACE OF AUTHORITY IN MATTERS OF RELIGIOUS BELIEF. By VINCENT HENRY STANTON, D.D., Fellow of Trinity Coll., Ely Prof. of Divinity, Cambridge. Cr. 8vo. 6s.

Swayne.—THE BLESSED DEAD IN PARADISE. Four All Saints' Day Sermons, preached in Salisbury Cathedral. By R. G. SWAYNE, M.A. *Crown 8vo. 3s. 6d.*

Twells.—COLLOQUIES ON PREACHING. By HENRY TWELLS, M.A., Honorary Canon of Peterborough. *Crown 8vo. 2s. 6d.*

Welldon.—THE FUTURE AND THE PAST. Sermons preached to Harrow Boys. By the Rev. J. E. C. WELLDON, M.A., Head Master of Harrow School. *Crown 8vo. 7s. 6d.*

Williams.—Works by the Rev. ISAAC WILLIAMS, B.D.
  A DEVOTIONAL COMMENTARY ON THE GOSPEL NARRATIVE, *Eight Vols. Crown 8vo. 5s. each. Sold Separately.*

  THOUGHTS ON THE STUDY OF THE HOLY GOSPELS.
  A HARMONY OF THE FOUR GOSPELS.
  OUR LORD'S NATIVITY.
  OUR LORD'S MINISTRY (Second Year).
  OUR LORD'S MINISTRY (Third Year).
  THE HOLY WEEK.
  OUR LORD'S PASSION.
  OUR LORD'S RESURRECTION.

  FEMALE CHARACTERS OF HOLY SCRIPTURE. A Series of Sermons, *Crown 8vo. 5s.*
  THE CHARACTERS OF THE OLD TESTAMENT. *Crown 8vo. 5s.*
  THE APOCALYPSE. With Notes and Reflections. *Crown 8vo. 5s.*
  SERMONS ON THE EPISTLES AND GOSPELS FOR THE SUNDAYS AND HOLY DAYS. *Two Vols. Crown 8vo. 5s. each.*

[*continued.*

A SELECTION OF THEOLOGICAL WORKS.

Williams.—Works by the Rev. ISAAC WILLIAMS, B.D.—*continued.*
PLAIN SERMONS ON CATECHISM. *Two Vols. Cr. 8vo.* 5s. *each.*
SELECTIONS FROM ISAAC WILLIAMS' WRITINGS. *Cr. 8vo.* 3s. 6d.
THE AUTOBIOGRAPHY OF ISAAC WILLIAMS, B.D., Author of several of the 'Tracts for the Times.' Edited by the Venerable Sir GEORGE PREVOST, as throwing further light on the history of the Oxford Movement. *Crown 8vo.* 5s.

Woodford.—Works by J. R. WOODFORD, D.D., Bishop of Ely.
THE GREAT COMMISSION. Addresses on the Ordinal. Edited, with an Introduction, by H. M. LUCKOCK, D.D. *Crown 8vo.* 5s.
SERMONS ON OLD AND NEW TESTAMENT SUBJECTS. Edited by H. M. LUCKOCK, D.D. *Two Vols. Crown 8vo.* 5s. *each.*

Wordsworth.
For List of Works by the late Christopher Wordsworth, D.D., Bishop of Lincoln, see Messrs. Longmans & Co.'s Catalogue of Theological Works, 32 pp. Sent post free on application.

Wordsworth.—Works by ELIZABETH WORDSWORTH, Principal of Lady Margaret Hall, Oxford.
ILLUSTRATIONS OF THE CREED. *Crown 8vo.* 5s.
THE DECALOGUE. *Crown 8vo.* 4s. 6d.
ST. CHRISTOPHER AND OTHER POEMS. *Crown 8vo.* 6s.

Wordsworth.—Works by CHARLES WORDSWORTH, D.D., D.C.L., Lord Bishop of St. Andrews, and Fellow of Winchester College.
ANNALS OF MY EARLY LIFE, 1806-1846. *8vo.* 15s.
ANNALS OF MY LIFE, 1847-1856. *8vo.* 10s. 6d.
PRIMARY WITNESS TO THE TRUTH OF THE GOSPEL, to which is added a Charge on Modern Teaching on the Canon of the Old Testament. *Crown 8vo.* 7s. 6d.

Younghusband.—Works by FRANCES YOUNGHUSBAND.
THE STORY OF OUR LORD, told in Simple Language for Children. With 25 Illustrations from Pictures by the Old Masters. *Crown 8vo.* 2s. 6d.
THE STORY OF THE EXODUS, told in Simple Language for Children. With Map and 29 Illustrations. *Crown 8vo.* 2s. 6d.

Printed by T. and A. CONSTABLE, Printers to Her Majesty,
at the Edinburgh University Press.

www.ingramcontent.com/pod-product-compliance
Lightning Source LLC
Chambersburg PA
CBHW021804230426
43669CB00008B/634